Spirituality in Education: Redefine Success as Rising Optimism, Peace & HAPPINESS

One to Five minutes Concentration Exercises for Replacing Negative Feelings with Positive Feelings by applying Choice, Discipline and Patience

Shiva Swati

SHIVA SWATI

DEDICATION

This book is dedicated to the children of Earth

Table of Contents

Note for the Reader

The easiest way to understand this book is to apply it on self. Each theory section is followed by a practical exercise. The exercises given need to be practiced to get the desired results from the theory sections.

The exercises are designed for thirty seconds to five minutes. *(If you cannot allot thirty seconds, start with practicing the exercise for one second. Time allotted is not as important as concentration allotted with willingness of convenience from the inner self)* .

It may be difficult for the beginners to finish the exercise in the given time if they get absorbed in understanding the theory. You can spend more time on each exercise given your convenience.

However, the faster you do the exercise, the less doubts you apply on the process and better is the result. Overtime, you will realize that you have developed enough focus to instantly detach from your routine worries and work on the allotted mental task. Reading and practicing one exercise a day would be more effective than overloading yourself.

Preface - Why is Spirituality Needed in Education?

The present education system has created a revolution in technology but has not solved problems which affect happiness directly like depression, psychological sickness, relationship breakdowns, corruption, terrorism etc.; hence, unrest and violence in society have increased. An understanding of what the soul needs from improving its efforts, is necessary to realize inner happiness as a direct outcome of effort and not as a side effect of success.

All technology innovations which we are so proud of as human beings, have been made only in the direction of improving external display or comforts without sufficient attention being given to our internal emotional and spiritual needs.

Happiness comes from satisfying the needs of emotional satisfaction along with acquiring bodily comforts. Becoming successful without feeling happy is like painting the walls of the house without the people feeling brighter. Happiness and good health are co-related... Good health can never be maintained by focusing on just the needs of material success and using the body as a projected image.

Since science only focuses on the outside world, just focusing on improvements in scientific development will never lead to evolution of peace and harmony within the soul or in society. A training in systematic understanding of emotional complexities needs to be inculcated with the same zeal as mathematical skills are taught.

Due to neglect of soul needs in the education curriculum, human development has failed to realize feelings of peace and contentment.

A focus on integration of soul needs along with material needs while teaching how to make choices in everyday life is essential to create peaceful adults. A training in integrated Emotional and Spiritual development is the only way to permanently increase peace and happiness in the world.

Though we blame everything else except our thinking patterns for the problems in our life , just focusing on grades/marks/ performance ability, success and money is the core negative thinking principle which has led to a lop-sided development of humanity wherein inner peace of the mind has been sacrificed for a need to perform due to external pressure.

This lop-sided development has led to creation of imbalanced individuals who have no training on how to resolve complex emotional issues and resort to violence or addictions to vent out frustrations in an attempt to find inner peace.

Human happiness cannot be created as a side-effect of success. You cannot get balanced, peaceful and happy adults by pursuing mechanical/academic success as the goal of education.

Mind patterns are set in childhood and are affected by mass culture which is affected by education, predominantly. Since, the focus of all education has been on becoming successful at the cost of neglecting training in development of peace and inner happiness, people are driven towards a rat race to earn success.

Training young minds to think that working mechanically for successful performance is all that is needed to be happy , makes them feel comfortable about ignoring complex emotional development , which actually aids human mind development towards evolving to be happy and healthy through the obstacles which adult life projects.

Children driven towards winning above being peaceful, start finding short-cuts to success which are manipulative and corrupt. A pattern of mass thinking has developed such that respect is measured by money. If you are not aiming at happiness or inner peace, money for success can be earned by being manipulative and corrupt more than by being good and helpful.

However, happiness and satisfaction come from a job well done whether it is acknowledged as successful conventionally, or not. Winning always is not necessary to be happy. Trial and error are common processes involved in research and inventions. Through the process of overcoming failure, happiness and satisfaction continue to motivate the person towards achieving success with satisfaction. For example, Thomas Edison continued to fail for thirty years before he finally created an electric bulb. Like him, students need to be trained to be motivated from within by a system of education which rewards the process of achieving satisfaction and not just the result.

A balanced training between inner satisfaction and outcome/ happiness vs. success ensures internal and external satisfaction even if the money earned is less than conventionally well defined. But, a pure focus on results/money/success leads to neglect of effort on feeling satisfaction. Peacefulness or freedom from anxiety

The need to never be peaceful is conditioned as a habit of thinking during schooling years, due to the stress on external good performance above inner peace. *Children are judged as being good or bad by external measures of success like school grades which later are replaced in adults by external measures of success like cars, clothes or jewels.*

However, getting good grades or performing well in sports or dance or music or art or earning good money in adult life does not lead to contentment in adult life. Children are always motivated to perform for pleasing society's norms of success and cannot focus on inner contentment.

Instead of just focusing on good external performance, mind patterns which focus on development of happiness and inner peace of mind have to be inculcated by redefining the education curriculum.

Negative thinking predominates mass thinking in today's world because people are not taught how to be peaceful in schools. This repeated pattern of negative thinking can be solved only by adding spiritual awareness to the concept of success; wherein development of peacefulness and compassion in children is as much awarded as good performance.

Children trained into being peaceful would make peaceful adults and create a peaceful world whereas restless children who are constantly asked to perform for success, make anxious adults and a restless world, which is prone to anger and violence.

A basic training in emotional management and the ability to create optimism with awareness ; are necessary to overcome all problems with a positive attitude and live a comfortable life; with the inner self being more in peace than being violent or angry.

If a connection to the subconscious mind and training in being peaceful are cultivated from childhood, escapism into depression or anger would not be the most natural route available to adults if marriages break down or finances collapse. Peace and emotional satisfaction will automatically rise in society and replace conflicts, anxiety and unrest.

The need for maintaining good health, optimism and contentment would spread as being as important as needs of education once a spiritual understanding of happiness is integrated along with being monetarily and mechanically successful in the education system.

Negative Thinking leads to ANARCHY in creation . You create what you do not desire to experience. Positive Thinking leads to harmony in creation where you create what you desire to experience

negative thinking creates random weeds in your life. Your life appears to be out of harmony , thoughts go everywhere, your body develops diseases, financial problems & relationship problems

positive thinking leads to balance in life where every aspect of life manifests as you desire. There is balance in money, relationship and health. Creation is of peace & harmony

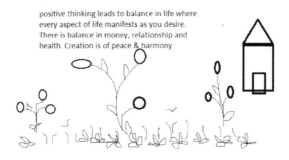

Chapter 2 - Peace & Happiness need to be targeted as Goals of Education

"Education is needed to be peaceful, optimistic and happy. The goal of all education is to help children find happiness in life. Education is not imparted just for being successful or earning money to support responsibilities. Education is given so that children learn to think and reason by using their brains more than their bodies, as distinguished from animals"

Education is encouraged in today's world for as many as can be reached by the literate society but peace and happiness are not as accredited. If you can afford it, have conducive family circumstances or are supported by the government, you do not opt to not get educated but you often take the choice to remain angry and become violent.

In today's world, money is considered as the measure of approval and success even if the process of earning money makes you negative. Anything that is paid for by money is supposed to be considered as motivational by the majority of people who identify happiness with consumable items and aim for satisfaction through buying cars, mobiles, jewels and clothes. However, happiness does not increase by buying products as much as it does not increase by playing with toys as children.

The factors which increase inner happiness are sidelined in the race for earning money which creates a society which is constantly complaining of unhappiness, depressions, diseases and misfortunes; only because the focus of thinking is on the negative aspects of evolution and creating short term satisfaction while ignoring the needs for peace and harmony.

This lop-sided focus of thinking towards using money as the measure of success arises from childhood, where success is measured by getting marks which gets transferred to earning money in adulthood.

There is much less attention given to feeling happy while working in childhood or feeling positive while earning money in adulthood. However, happiness is a result of accumulation of positive feelings which release positive hormones in the body, which, subsequently, create satisfaction in the soul.

In contrast with the presumption that accredited success automatically leads to happiness; the feelings of happiness, contentment, joy & excitement which arise during working in any activity are the key ingredients for the continuation of satisfaction after the job is done.

The outcome of any activity is felt as positive if the feelings being pursued during the act are more positive than negative, on an average. If, during work, compromise is more than satisfaction, people are bound to feel depressed as negative hormones will increase more than positive hormones in the body.

Though there are several good effects of the present education system, there is negligible attention given to creation of positive feelings which would lead to evolution of consciousness towards a more peaceful world. The inadequate method of measurement of happiness by measuring success as good marks is spreading negative thinking by its excessive focus on quantitative development over development of qualitative understanding that overtime, leads to positive thinking in human consciousness.

With increasing emptiness in hearts and violence in the world, there is an urgent need to minimize the negativity arising as side effect of the enforcement of education; for accentuating the positive benefits.

Side Effects of the Present Education System

The education system of today glorifies success over happiness; leading to a complex situation wherein people try to be successful to be happy; but do not attain the happiness they seek from their efforts through being successful and hence, become disillusioned overtime, leading to increasing depressions and violence in societies.

As long as success is pursued blindly by promoting competition in childhood, it justifies increasing of happiness in self by reducing happiness of others; thus justifying corruption and promotion of inequalities amongst adults.

Anger and negative feelings amongst those defeated rise and the energy of jealousy/unhappiness spreads and dilutes the positive efforts of the successful; because all human energy is connected. Jealousy, wars and manipulations which ravage the defeated minds, often create more harm than the good effects created by success.

To understand why success has become important over happiness, we need to understand how education evolved from a need of survival carried over from our animal ancestors.

Evolution of Education – From Animal Mindset to a Human Mindset

Education represents the development of human life over animal life, and is the most important factor which distinguishes human beings from animals.

Animals often feel helpless against circumstances because their brain is less developed, unlike the human brain. Animals cannot grow resources as they live only in the present moment and have no future visions, no ability to abstract words from pictures or analyze in logical or abstract steps. Animals cannot reason about the WHYs or think of the HOWs. Since, animals cannot read or write or imagine/ co-create abundance, animals have genuine fears of survival.

Hence, animals are justified in racing for survival and killing for competition for reasons such as fear, food or self-defense.

However, human beings are not justified in becoming competitively brutal, racing for money or using violence because their minds have the capacity to sustain the body without using rudimentary methods of survival as the animals use.

The development of literacy represents the complexifying of human existence over animal existence in all areas of life. Literacy has improved life associated with survival, production of resources, money, counting, exchange of goods and services, creating technology, inventions, and has also, led to increased development of the creative brain in areas other than the concept of surviving in the animal world. The spread of education has facilitated spiritual development of the brain and manifested portals of expression such as painting, dance, music, evolution of relationships, literature, history, geography etc.

However, though, education has evolved technology, it has remained primitive by intention and animal-like in its execution. The stress on competition, scarcity consciousness and compromising in fear for survival has had negative effects on general peacefulness in society. The development of literacy has not been not able to neutralize the need to overpower others by increasing optimism, compassion and peacefulness more than the need for negative thinking and helplessness.

The present debate is between the opposing thinking patterns of a survival consciousness and an evolutionarily higher abundance consciousness which has a higher positive thought frequency. Positive thinking seeks to spread education such that the negative effects of competition are transcended by a focus on abundance & benefits of human life over animal life with the understanding that animal-like needs of violence and competition are harmful and reduce spread of happiness in human terms.

The evolution of education should be such that it aids in development of peace in the minds of people by facilitating peacefulness in individual consciousness which aids in spreading of happiness as an energy flowing from one to several, in mass consciousness. This requires an understanding of the factors which led to the initial expansion of education and realizing that those circumstances no longer hold true, with deliberate awareness.

Evolutionary History of Education

Charles Darwin's research as published in his book " The Origin Of Species " , propagated the theory of *Survival of the Fittest* , which suggests that animals survive in the jungles by killing and defeating others less capable than the fittest.

Animals killed because they depended on scarce resources. **If you did not kill as an animal, you were amongst those who were eaten.** Competition evolved as a tool of survival because animals genuinely needed to develop competitive fighting skills to survive.

However, due to the repetitive energy cycles which govern all energy movement in the universe, these dominant thought cycles continued to repeat though external circumstances kept changing as humans evolved from animals.

Human beings continued to believe in the illusion that if you are not a winner, you would be a victim without any genuine cause. Though, there was no animal-like associated helplessness arising from an inability to grow resources, **definitions of success and power were blindly carried over from the animal mind-set.**

Success in the animal world, came from defeating others because resources were not enough for all; and they could not grow resources as human beings could; but success in the human world was falsely assumed to be that which came from defeating others wherein scarcity was artificially created for fun or learning.

Just as power in the animal world was equated with violence and killing, *power* in the human world was defined by emotional bullying/ killing of the optimistic human spirit. .

Therefore, success and power in the human world, as blindly imitated

22

from the animal world, were defined by a survival instinct and not by an increase in inner peace or happiness.

Thus, it came about that, as human beings advanced from animals, their bodies evolved but the thinking patterns remained stuck at rudimentary energy cycles where the belief was that *'you have to competitively crush others to dominate '*.It was firmly believed that competition was necessary to survive as it had been when human ancestors were animals.

Hence, though teeth were replaced by guns as the brain evolved from being animal-like to human-like, the technological improvement did not erase the primitive need to kill to survive. The concept of the 'enemy 'and 'a need to kill another's spirit to survive oneself' continued to be accepted as gospel.

This crux of fear based thinking has not changed though human civilization has evolved technologically. A vicious circle of scarcity and competition has resulted as a circuitous chain of evolution. *Circumstances of life manifest in alignment with dominant thinking cycles. Since there was a belief in scarcity of resources, it manifested such that human beings genuinely feel trapped in cycles of scarcity wherein the scarcity is inappropriately advertised by excessive focus on comfort, greed, fear, poverty, future dangers and traditional criteria of right & wrong. Usually, individual consciousness is ruled over by mass consciousness and we allow others to decide how life should be.*

The education system has developed an imitative mechanism of learning such that, the cycle of feeling helpless individually and as a mass, has continued automatically from the competitive animal's mind-set. In alignment with the laws of automatic repetition of energy cycles, instead of promoting meaningfulness and peace in life, education has been imparted in a way which has fueled energies of compromise, helplessness and negative competition.

Animals felt helpless without competing because their intelligence was limited to grabbing food and shelter whereas human beings feel helpless without competition and bitterness, because of repeated patterns of thinking being carried over from animal conditioning.

Logic is ignored by repetitive energy/ thought cycles until it is imposed by deliberate changes in the super-structure made by a higher, more positive consciousness.

The human soul is a co-creator unlike the animal soul which is a passive receiver. Therefore, the responsibility of creation of happiness, peace and sufficient resources for survival is as much human as God's in the human world. We cannot blame God or external factors for our problems just as the primitive man could not blame God for not giving rain on time.

Abundance can be created in the human world by choice, unlike the animal world which is dependent on luck and rain. The imaginative/ abstract / creative brain power which human beings have and animals do not have, automatically places humans on a higher realm of feeling intricacies of life and being in control. Human beings can create abundance of happiness with a disciplined focus of the mind on the positive aspects of life. Inequalities in distribution of wealth can be overcome by practical application of abundance consciousness in everyday thinking.

Just as rain can be created through manipulating external factors, happiness can be accessed by manipulating internal dominant emotional focus by choice. But as long as we think that we are basically animals, helpless and dependent on external circumstances for our happiness, we would continue fighting over survival needs as animals do and leave happiness to chance.

Instead of priding over our animal instinct, we need to

acknowledge ourselves as a more evolved, higher dimensional human race , being more intelligent than animals are and having the ability to create happiness, health, food, goods & services by practicing spiritual awareness and understanding how our feelings impact reality through the action of the Universal Laws of Soul Vibration.

Abundance vs. Scarcity Consciousness

Human beings have evolved above animals in terms of physical bodies but they now, need to move above animalistic survival based thinking; wherein the *'survival instinct* 'is replaced by an *'abundance instinct'*; such that a belief in abundance of resources replaces the competitive negativity arising due to a belief in scarcity of resources.

Abundance Consciousness is a mind-set which deliberately focuses on the blessings of life - on all those good aspects of life which reflect love, peace or good health with the belief that contentment will grow in abundance in the future. For example, a focus on feeling gratitude for being generally healthy is *abundance consciousness* whereas a focus on the painful areas of the body and feeling generally unhealthy because of minor problems is *Scarcity Consciousness*. Similarly, a focus on feeling wealthy because your necessities are being met by your work/life choices is *abundance consciousness* whereas a focus on all the goods which are in the market and which you want to buy but cannot buy, is *scarcity consciousness*.

People have been trained into focusing on the scarcities of life, due to the traditional belief that pain/the negative situation has to be focused upon to be fixed. However, a focus on pain creates sadness and a feeling of failure.

Focusing on failure does not help to fix a negative situation. To resolve a painful situation, focus needs to be on clearing the errors and healing the negative aspect of life with appropriate measures while channeling the remaining energy on fueling the positive aspects of life.

Metaphorically, if you have failed in one subject but have passed in all others, your focus needs to be not on sadness of failing but on the positive learning attached to the sadness of having failed. Instead of feeling emotionally negative because you failed, you need to concentrate on the positive emotional solution of the problem. You can either choose to focus on passing the one subject in which you have failed or on learning detachment by ignoring the failure as insignificant or continue your efforts such that your overall confidence grows.

Traditionally, suffering has been focused upon by choice as *scarcity consciousness* was predominant. It was believed that suffering is inevitable and has to be borne. However, suffering makes you continuously focus on the area of life where you have failed without adequate attention being given to fuel optimism which is necessary to overcome suffering. Evolution of consciousness entails that a choice to focus upon happiness predominates over sadness, with conscious awareness of those areas of life where there is abundance so that the faith in positive life force grows.

The need to curtail indulgence in happiness arises from a generalized assumption that resources are scarce & won't grow overtime. Hence, compromise on happiness in the present is necessary to be happy in the future. Excessive focus on future with a fear of scarcity leads to creation of feelings of deprivation in the present. Suffering in silence manifests pessimism, hatred, anger & suppression overtime, that lead to a need to vent out frustration through aggression, whenever an opportunity arises. If people do not use violence externally, they become sick internally as the suppressed violence is subconsciously vented out by harming the self through indulging in negative thinking & escapist addictive habits which create negative hormones in the body.

Abundance consciousness means having a thinking pattern which is patient and optimistic. *A **consciousness of abundance** leads to* reduction of greed arising out of a fear that there will be scarcity in the future. The future is expected to be happier than the present without worries being fueled as the belief is that *'there is plenty and always will be; hence, there is freedom of choice to be positive because the difficulties will pass away overtime'*.

Abundance consciousness fuels energies upon the best aspects of self more than the worst ; whereas scarcity/poverty consciousness is the awareness of the worst aspects of life with the belief that ' *there is scarcity and always will be; hence, hoarding of resources is required in the present as difficulties will always remain and worsen in the future.* '

Scarcity consciousness arises due to a shortage of money to buy resources and not due to an inability to grow resources. Resources are available in large magnitudes today in the human technologically advanced money based economy. If you have money, you can buy anything which is held to be competitively scarce.

The scarcity or helplessness which is felt in everyday life is a problem of Poverty/ helplessness Consciousness which is a vibrational manifestation problem carried over from the primitive mindset. In the human world, the scarcity manifests due to a persistent focus on fear of losing which creates an unequal distribution of incomes, goods & services. There is no real scarcity but scarcity is maintained to balance power equations as in the animal world where there was a belief that the strong have to eat the weak in order to rule as only the fittest can survive. The theory of ' *Survival of the fittest* ' explains the need for measures to maintain monopolies and rich-poor class differences at the cost of bearing unhappiness amongst those deprived.

Energy travels from one being to another and unhappiness of the souls who are unjustly treated passes onto reduce the happiness of souls who feel powerful in the form of dis-obedience, rebellions, curses, conflicts, strikes etc. Since, animals do not feel poor/ rich, this emotional quality of happiness is sidelined in a blindly imitated competitive struggle for survival. Due to the Law of Repetition, governing life cycles, human beings inadvertently, continue to behave like animals who want to be powerful even if it makes them negative/ anxious/ sick.

The evolution of resources from primitive times to modern times, shows the tremendous technological progress humanity has achieved but the *scarcity consciousness* remains because fear remains in the traditional mind. Due to the need to maintain power structures in self-defense, and a blind belief in helplessness, the means of distribution of surplus resources are curtailed by motives of monopolization, autocracy and corruption; which uphold individual profiting over mass welfare. Energy exchange is biased towards material display of power by advertising and glamour. In fact, surplus resources are thrown away in developed countries because of market manipulative strategies of capitalism.

Hence, the solution to happiness is to break the animal mind-set of divisions where individuals struggle for survival to save their single power equations, at the cost of some profiting over several others or one winning where several lose the race. Awareness needs to be developed that life is no longer a race or a struggle for survival but an artistic expression of the co-creator which can prosper with differences of opinions.

Surplus and happiness for all would grow in a variety of ways when efforts are made to replace the need to COMPETE with a need to COMPLETE.

Happiness cannot arrive until the scarcity conditioning is discarded with training in the realization that the problem in the human world today is not of scarcity of resources but of inequality of distribution. As long as competitive capitalism is the model of growth, people hold back their surplus, creativity, talent, goods and services because of fear of losing money and not because there is inability to grow more . People inhibit their abilities to spread love and happiness instead of using their surplus to complete other's deficits.

Competition blocks ease of travel of resources from surplus areas to deficit areas. This inhibition indirectly blocks the spread of creative and productive energy, thus slowing down further technological growth and soul evolution.

Scarcity continues to manifest unchecked, because of fear of losing, and starts being inculcated from school years. This conditioned fear of losing makes children competitive, restless, aggressive and violent more than compassionate, content, peaceful and happy; as they start behaving like animals competitively fighting for resources in the jungle

Human society needs more minds seeking to complete deficits in happiness by helping each other than minds which are competitively successful. Instead of competing for scarce resources, human beings need to be trained from childhood to complement each other and work to complete each other's deficiencies; so that resources increase in abundance for all involved.

The much needed abilities of sharing & compassion, which are lacking in human world today due to lack of focus , can be technically developed through a modified education structure which stresses on developing human skills like patience and empathy along with academic skills, so that positive thinking becomes a part of routine individual repertoire. The spread of positive thinking increases abundance consciousness in several automatically.

Unlike food, happiness spreads when you spread happiness to others. Food reduces once it is consumed but happiness increases once it is consumed and distributed. Originally, happiness was identified with having food & shelter, as it was so in the animal world.

Hence, there was fear that happiness would reduce if we spread the goods. But, human beings do not identify happiness with just consumable items anymore. Human evolution has an increasing hunger for emotionally positive frequencies which increase by receiving satisfaction in all aspects of life, not only food or clothing or shelter. The advancing soul has an increasing need for love, acknowledgement and self-respect to be happy.

Empirically, it has been proven that human beings could never be content if they just received food & shelter as animals seemed. The slave cult was abolished because human beings needed more than food & shelter to be happy in routine life, unlike the animals. The slaves received only food & shelter in exchange for work, but they rebelled whereas the animals continued to work in the same mound. Hence, animal laws of scarcity cannot be blindly superimposed on human beings as people can get starved of happiness if focus is given merely to food & shelter

Happiness grows through investing efforts in mutual trade which focuses on devising methods of developing abundance for all. Happiness or well-being does not increase through investing in competitive games, wars & terrorism which provide short term diversions at the cost of wastage of resources in ego based conflicts of territories/ religions or nations.

Human civilization has already suffered severe trauma for running away from emotional problems and resorting to wars to resolve ego based arguments. The huge amounts of energy and money invested in wars and defense weapons can, now, be avoided if investment on emotional management is given a priority over competitive sports; which subsequently manifests as war games played at macro levels.

Happiness spreads while being happy oneself and not by sacrificing needs of love, creativity or satisfaction for future peacefulness. While indulging in greed is not needed to increase happiness, a focus on contentment is necessary to feel abundance in life. Present feelings multiply over time and positive thinking generates more positivity overtime, while feeling sad, compromised or negatively competitive creates more unhappiness over the long run with bad effects on health & inherent peacefulness.

Abundance consciousness spreads happiness from one to several through words spoken & feelings generated which increase optimism, and open doorways to experience love, creativity & passion. Complaining about survival, in terms of whether you will get food / shelter or not, is a primitive thinking habit which needs to be deliberately discontinued and replaced with optimistic thinking. By default, "**Abundance consciousness**" motivates positive thinking while "**Poverty/Scarcity Consciousness**"promotes negative thinking.

Hence, a focus on developing **abundance consciousness** needs to supersede **poverty/scarcity/war consciousness** while training young minds. Children need to be trained into thinking that there is enough for all and always will be. Beliefs manifest reality .Vibrations are created in alignment with the feelings focused upon.

Scarcity or feelings of deprivation are created more by the habit of focusing on fear or greed than a real scenario in the Modern world.

Very often, individuals do not give charity of surplus as much as they can because there is no means to reach those who need due to lack of opportunities of fair distribution. Individuals want to open their wings and spread happiness in the modern world, but are blocked by a traditional mass super structure which believes in scarcity of resources and hence , there are channels created for saving for wars & self –defense, but not for distribution of excess resources.. Once opportunity is created, sharing of surplus would be a preferred option to indulging in excessive of clothes/drugs/food/ cars/ jewelry, as it would be more satisfying for the soul.

In contrast with abundance consciousness, a belief in having LESS compared to others, creates sadness in self and the sadness spreads like a virus spreading. The energy of sadness spreads faster than the energy of happiness because negative electrons have a higher magnetic content than positive electrons.

In our poverty conscious world, sadness of one person makes several people cry in despair, and believe more in the individual's debilitated state. Newspapers and social media thrive on accentuating negative thinking.

Feelings of helplessness and despair spread in an uncontrolled manner because of the traditionally honored belief of needing to focus on the suffering of human life. Sadness and helplessness are repetitively aggravated by focusing on problems, more than on accomplishments. A choice to be *not content* is ingrained in the human mind-set by traditional thinking of focusing on past suffering; instead of on the thinking patterns which help in overcoming suffering.

From an energy/ soul's perspective, humanity, as a race is infected by cancer of the spleen. Metaphorically, just as a human being develops cancer by focusing on anger & helplessness, mass consciousness is infected with the virus of helplessness, due to a rigid belief in unchangeable suffering. In spite of huge improvements in living standards, human health is destroying itself due to inappropriately focusing on the negative energy that there is lack of sufficient immunity against difficulties, which creates an internal dominant focus on sadness. The cancer which , affects humanity today and spreads terrorism, aggression & wars , is created by excessively focusing on anger , rejection & despair at an individual or mass scale.

This illusion of helplessness is created by focus on injustice more than on improvements. The appearance of negativity would reduce when the fear of scarcity dies in individuals and surplus of goods is spread to the poor who reflect lack of abundance with educational efforts made to raise their vibrational frequency to receive and manifest abundance.

From the perspective of the evolving individual human, there is too much food, too many fashions, too many medicines, too much work and too many choices available in the modern world. The feeling that there is **too much** is increasing as individual humans strive to strike a balance between need and greed, with the understanding that greed is harmful in the long run for maintaining peace, good health or optimism. People are trying to learn how to say NO to excessive surplus of resources because there is so much to choose from.

However, feelings of scarcity continue to rule over our subconscious minds because the traditional models of growth based on the principle of scarcity of resources, have not been revamped in tune with the changing times.

Though news about despair & loss pays more money as negativity is absorbed faster due to its magnetic content, spreading a negative mass consciousness spreads waves of sadness to all. The evolutionary shift in human consciousness towards a qualitatively better life for all, would be facilitated when focus of education, media & newspapers shifts towards depicting positive aspects of individual lives or the growing abundance of the human race, which has already overcome several centuries of struggle to arrive at a consciously abundant world.

Happiness increases only if positivity is allowed to be the dominating energy in the mind by choice and with practice of positive thinking self -help exercises, which reduce the habit of the mind to automatically slope downwards towards fueling the energy of negative thinking.

In alignment with the rising abundance of resources in the modern industrial world, an inbuilt **abundance consciousness** would ensure that methods of distribution are created such that compassion, empathy and sharing rule over monopoly and competitive money making games. When mass consciousness is positive, waves of happiness spread for all. Increasing happiness for others, increases positivity in self.

Walls of division have been created from the primitive times onwards when fear of losing resources was paramount. Due to habits of continued negative thinking, people remained trapped in feelings of deprivation. Racism & nationalist feelings were promoted in school syllabi.

Competitiveness and violence still continue to be a major tool of survival used as is evident from the stature of armies which all countries maintain to defend themselves from '*enemies*'.

In today's advancing world of the internet and world wide unification of thoughts, there is no continuing real need for creating national boundaries for safeguarding resources of food and shelter, as was in the primitive era.

The development of **abundance consciousness** would be much easier if countries work on international trade with peace, without the need to spread terrorism, threats & fear. However, almost one-third of financial resources of national governments are spent on defense expenditures which can be used for development of health, education & peace in the masses.

God represents peace and harmony in every religion but our education system stresses more on differences in regions and religions than unanimity and thus, fails to teach that all religions essentially uphold the same principles of love, understanding and Oneness.

The concept of nationalism creates mental walls, and promotes egotist racism, which leads to inequalities in distribution of food, services and benefits of technology. Economic inequalities are subsequently used by religious leaders who instigate the poor against the rich by quoting religion as the reason for disharmony/war whereas the underlying reason is always a need to amass more wealth for self over others, coming from the animal-mindset. People of every religion need economic welfare equally but the need to compete makes people brand their own God as superior to another, thus creating a need for anger/ violence.

Education and literacy are meaningless if they do not lead to creation of a happier and more peaceful world. If an increase in overall happiness was targeted instead of the need to be superior to others, there would be no need to glorify the self over others and create economic inequalities to feel powerful.

Differences in religious worship are natural and have developed as language differences have developed in different regions but these differences are superficial and need to be ignored than prioritized, to promote a peaceful and harmonious world where different breeds can live together as an unanimously evolving consciousness.

When belief in having surplus increases with faith in overall abundance, happiness spreads as insecurity of each individual reduces. Each person feels safe about spreading happiness and helping others as accentuating welfare of each other increases mutual satisfaction, happiness, peace, faith & optimism. Contributing towards growth of positive energy in another's life raises the frequency of positive energy in self while creating vibrations of abundance which spread peacefulness to several others.

Peace in the world is a direct outcome of individuals feeling at peace in their own lives; as the more restless and competitive individuals feel, the more are tensions and wars created at the mass level. Mass consciousness is a sum total of individual consciousness.

Change begins from the individual and reaches the masses where it can be accepted or discarded. To evolve to a happier and more peaceful world, the rudimentary mind-set of using force & violence needs to be replaced by deliberate training given to individual young minds to feel abundant and not competitively judged; so that the whole structure is motivated to think differently and evolution speeds up as attempts are focused upon completing each other's deficits more than competing with each other's talents.

Shiva Swati

Chapter 3 - Impact of Education on Cycles of Life

Situations which create trauma or happiness in life, are created by previous circumstances which influence thinking. Thinking Patterns create energy cycles which govern life through generating positive or negative vibrations

Education given in childhood influences patterns of thinking in adulthood. Positive or negative frequencies of thinking are conditioned through repeated self-talk or advise given in childhood. The emotional formulas for tackling problems which help the child escape or evolve, are subsequently implemented by adults while dealing with problems of everyday life.

Education is meant to help in problem-solving so that emotional intelligence can be applied in areas where mathematical intelligence, linguistic intelligence, sports , dancing or activities like karate, do not help in creating happiness.

The motive of education is to create a happy and peaceful life. However, instead of creating a peaceful life, the educational design followed in the modern, industrial world is such that it manifests a reverse cycle of thinking where negative vibrations are increasingly reinforced. As a result, life becomes difficult for children as they move into adulthood. Children become more anxious and aggressive in a competitive educational system, instead of becoming emotionally wiser and peaceful.

Difficulties add up because children grow up with a sustained focus on compromise, as the motivation for education is created by focusing on *what is missing.*

A Law of Repetition operates energy cycles of life in the universe. Energy which influences life patterns is released through the electric impulses generated while feeling an experience, as will be explained in more detail in chapters to follow. Children learn to feel more by imitation than by preaching. Because of a general focus on suffering in the world, and a need to be materialistically successful, children are conditioned into thinking that '*sacrifice of present happiness for future happiness* 'is essential to be happy, which creates a need for feeling sad, by fashion.

The pre-dominant feelings of sacrifice and compromise which you focus upon in childhood keep repeating themselves in increasing intensity as life force rotating in cycles of energy movement. **A focus on *what is missing* trains young minds to repeatedly focus on deprivation instead of on contentment and fulfilment.**

A pattern of repetitive negative thinking results from a constant need to feel worried instead of focusing on being content with that which is positive about life. Complaints are subconsciously enumerated over the blessings. Peacefulness evades the being, as anxiety rules internal energy circuits.

Contentment and subsequently, peacefulness can come in mass consciousness and in the individual, only by focusing on positive aspects of life more than the negative. Positive energy increases by absorbing the happiness from natural surroundings, and by focusing on accomplishments rather than on failures in everyday life.

However, due to a pre-conditioned expectation to continuously perform and improve, there is insufficient time given to absorb and imbibe what has already been learnt; as more and more information is piled on young minds, which remains undigested. Half of the information which is taught to children becomes irrelevant in adult life but takes up a disproportionately large amount of time in childhood.

The same energy used in the enforcement of discipline for teaching academics can be partly redirected instead on practicing meditation and developing positive thinking exercises which would help improve health and optimism in adult attitudes. *Instead, priority time is wasted on teaching general facts which are meaningless from the perspective of training young minds moving towards emotional challenges of adulthood.*

This blind obedience to authoritative thinking which develops in childhood results in blind imitation of ritualistic thinking, fashion trends and addictive behaviors in adulthood. Several people choose imbalanced relationships, food habits and life styles only because they feel compelled to continue mechanically without feeling emotionally fulfilled.

Often, adults encounter subconscious fear when they choose to go against society's norms because childhood minds are pressurized to obey by using abuse, fear and competition as the teaching forces. If children refuse to learn, they are reprimanded and punished for not choosing to improve as per the required authoritarian directive or advised school curriculum.

Education needs to be an ongoing process of participation rather than a test of discipline, facts or computing ability. However, instead of allowing original thinking to evolve in different ways, uniformity of thinking is encouraged. If children question authority directives in family or in school, they are deprived of a regular flow of love and praise.

The deprivation factor of needing to learn out of fear of losing love, which is used for training the so-called *right thinking* that is often outdated with the current technological/social context, makes children think that the world is a negative place to be in where continuous compromise and sacrifices are demanded and justice is not given, as it should be.

Teachers constantly feel frustrated and helpless as children rebel because they are forced to ensure discipline at the cost of development of intelligent questioning thinking. Schools have to function like armies but the same obedience cult does not help to resolve complex work or emotional relationships in adult life.

This negative mind-set creates anger and restlessness in young minds which leads to aggressive outbursts in adulthood. If the blind belief in a traditional, rigid scarcity - based doctrine is removed, minor changes can easily revise the educational design so that children enjoy learning and find it meaningful by using the applications in their everyday life.

Yet, though several understand the gaps in the system, individual attempts to initiate change are suppressed and negative thinking is allowed to grow, in an attempt to keep the structure intact. While young children need the *deprivation factor* as a motivation to grow, the same negative focus continued over the years creates diseases as the repetitive focus continues to remain on the deprivation factors in life, instead of on contentment. Angry/ depressed/sick adults emerge from enthusiastic minds suppressed in childhood.

The core focus on constantly searching for "What is Missing", is fertilized as a seed of negative thinking which leads to the development of a tree of negative thinking that grows with several branches of 'what is missing' in every area of life. Children conditioned into thinking negatively remain dis-satisfied in every sphere of life in adulthood. The seed of thought is fertilized by constant repetition of the same feeling of focusing on what is missing with an obligation for a need to improve.

For a tree of peacefulness, good health and happiness to grow, instead; mind training needs to be given to dissolve the negative energy stuck on roots of thinking.

Once negative thinking spreads from a suffering individual to mass consciousness, from micro to macro levels, it multiplies suffering for all .A negative focus of thinking, leads to inherent corruption, dis-satisfaction as the dominating internal focus , criticism of optimism, impatience, fear of losing fame or surface reputation, complaining attitudes, and mass aggression in the form of terrorisms and wars. As the inner disharmony surfaces up, individual bodies face diseases/abuse and the planet Earth throws up suppressed negative energy to restore its inner positive balance in the form of floods, epidemics or violence.

Once the dirt shows up on the surface, the authorities desperately seek to erase the dismal picture without looking into the cause, which arises from the roots of the educational system. .

A sustained focus on the need to improve physical accomplishments at the cost of sacrifice of inner understanding, which begins in childhood as a side-effect of the general focus on *'what is missing '*, leads to development of greed overruling need, in adulthood as the mind-set that seeks continuous improvements moves to a *cycle of greed* which redefines 'need' as an endless, disproportionate craving for more. Greed leads to restlessness, obesity, alcoholism and corruption which lead to rising frustrations and anger in mass consciousness.

Instead of correcting flaws in the educational structure, there is a search for *Who to blame* when conflicts escalade. Subsequently, the visible flaws of government policies, terrorists and criminals are blamed almost as arbitrarily, as famines are blamed for lack of water supply.

Metaphorically, just as the primitive man passed responsibility of every problem on the rains, in the modern day, the government policies of the day are conveniently blamed for all unrest in society while individuals escape responsibility. However, the government as a macro unit, reflects the problems faced by individuals as micro units.

Once the individual mind's dominant vibrational point is set on an energy cycle of being negative & restless, governments cannot control violence by sweeping dirt from the surface. Peacefulness is eroded by focusing on negative aspects of life and complaining about injustice, without understanding that there is virus in the roots of behavior.

Children learn more by imitation of adult behavior than preaching. Since domestic violence, bullying, abuse or threats, continue as tools for teaching children , violence in adulthood or bullying is an accepted norm when these children grow up to be leaders. Economic dominance is used to threaten other nationalities because it is traditionally assumed that competition is necessary as Earth is a scarcely resourced planet, wherein bullying & monopolization help to survive.

Logical methods of reasoning are ignored as violence and competition offer faster methods of achieving an outcome, even though it does not change inner mind-sets to positive. Criminals and terrorists are created because there is an inherent belief that competitive violence helps in instilling obedience. Wars are planned for by competing armies, being maintained at the cost of sacrifice of emotional/ human development.

Even entertainment in the modern world revolves around competitive sports, competitive dance programs and the paradigm of defeating the weak. People waste hours to relax by watching cricket and soccer matches because the hormonal ups and downs created by competitive situations, work as addictions. There can be far greater relaxation created if the same amount of time and energy was invested on meditation, sleeping or just being in a peaceful or positive state of neutral detachment. Relaxing the sense organs helps in improving health and happiness while watching sports or eating junk foods have negative effects on being peaceful or healthy. Yet, the war games are created and cultivated by adults enjoying the virtual emotional killing as happens in video games.

The same war mind-set spreads to real life from the sports field, and creates religious fights, terrorism and crime thrills. The more criminals and terrorists are killed, the more they get created further as the focus of individual thinking remains on enjoying competition.

The abusers who exert negative power to win success, feel most anxious, bitter and unhealthy themselves. However, abuse continues to rule as competitive success is glorified – be it negatively exerted or positively responsible. Just as children get away by obtaining good marks through cheating, adults get away by obtaining power by side-lining ethics and betraying mass welfare.

There is no distinction made between negative power and positive power as minds are conditioned during childhood by the educational structure which does not teach a distinction between positive power (*success with understanding , satisfaction and happiness*) and negative power *(success without contentment which reduces peacefulness or happiness).*

A balanced mind would aim at addressing both spiritual and material needs so that happiness and health improve in self and others; but a competitive mind aims at success even if the pursuit deteriorates health and peace of mind for self and everyone involved. .

However, due to lack of training in schools, the spiritual aspect of life is ignored as irrelevant. The mind which is trained on the basis of competitive success fuels the need to defeat and kill others to survive itself, as an individual, a country or a religious sect.

There is no awareness of concepts like Spiritual Evolution, Emotional Management and Emotional Intelligence, because the spiritual or emotional aspects of life are neglected in mass education systems. The child's mind trained on constantly seeking improvement, is never allowed to be different than uniform.

Since, it is unusual behavior to be peaceful or content , training in peace and happiness is left to a trial and error process instead of being customized by using methods of Emotional Management which has several techniques for creating happiness , as a deliberate choice just as good health is created as a deliberate discipline . However, the total focus of education remains on teaching technical, mathematical or scientific skills which makes children feel like non emotional robots obeying masters.

Adults who start thinking like robots become mechanical in approach, feel sad and empty in all free moments and usually suffer from bad health but do not understand why there is negativity in their life. Robots can only obey or feel lifeless and when human beings are trained as robots are, they become as clueless about how to create happiness by using love, care and positive thinking. This insistence of obedience over teaching emotional evolution creates imbalanced adults who escape into shopping, sports, alcoholism or eating fatty foods; whenever any emotional problem comes up; instead of applying an organized emotional problem solving process to resolve issues.

Deliberate escapism from emotional conflicts release negative hormones which subsequently creates diseases in the body and anxiety problems in individuals. (*The healing aspect of Emotional Management is given in my books: A Course in Emotional Management & the Creation of Happiness: the Energy War, a soul's perspective*)

However, in the modern era, just as famines have been controlled by water management through a focus on technological development, the 'famines' of contentment and happiness need to be controlled by training children to be content and peaceful as a part of school curriculum from childhood..

Children need to be trained to sleep more, rest more and do activities at intervals so that focus is on quality of performance rather than the quantity of work. Training in peace needs to be cultivated by disciplining children to sit and be silent for at least a minute in every hour so that the mind gets into habituated to being in peace with practice.

Quality of performance automatically increases multi-fold when inner free space is created in the subconscious mind as a deliberate practice.

However, restlessness, escapism and poor performance are created when children are forced to get up early, and march to school, in fear of getting beaten up. While getting up early is refreshing for some, it can be harmful for others as different people have different sleep cycles, unlike animals who have uniform sleep cycles. Children need to be allowed to get up naturally or cajoled to awaken after the recommended norm of 8-10 hours of sleep.

When children sleep late and are forced to get up early, there is inadequate sleep time given. Inadequate rest releases restless states of feeling which releases negative hormones in the body that lead to creation of the energy of unhappiness. Forced intervention to break natural resting states as in early morning time of deep sleep, sends a fear message to the subconscious mind that *"You cannot rest. You have to perform to succeed to be happy or you will lose on happiness in the future. If you do not get up, you will be beaten up* '.

The first feeling which a person gets up with sets the tone of the day. If you can get up after adequate sleep and feel relaxed, you would smile upon awakening with a positive feeling and have a thankful note in the mind. Since the first feeling of the day sets the emotional tone/frequency for the day, when you get up feeling non pressurized, you would focus on positive aspects of life through the whole day automatically; whereas if you get up with a negative feeling, in pressure & dis-contentment, your inner energy cycles would drift towards feeling negative and discontented the whole day.

The obligation to perform by demanding uniform awakening patterns, creates negative frequencies in the mind which create several types of emotional dis-harmonies during the day that reduce quality of work performance and happiness.

To train the mind to be positive, it is essential to get up with positive feelings in the morning. A child's mind has to be conditioned into releasing positive hormones by making sure that s/he gets up with a smile in the morning and notices all the good things around; instead of being grumpy and sullen; which is inherently because he is forced to get up from a resting brain state.

Since the adult mind gets conditioned into patterns of thinking from childhood, a focus on teaching *Fear* and *Compromise* in childhood, to be happy in the future; perpetuates a cycle of *Fear* and *Compromise* in adulthood; wherein adults keep feeling compromised over feeling happy in the hope that happiness would come in the future; which never does; as the cycle keeps rotating on the axis of compromise.

By the Laws of Soul Vibrations in the universe, feelings are the energy vibrations which revolve the key to creation of reality.

For example, if you are an adult, you can start to test the process of creating deliberate soul vibrations by choice, so that you can teach the same process to children.

Start by trying the following exercise:

Practical Exercise 1 (PE 3.1)

When you wake up, silence your mind by deliberately side-lining negative feelings and focusing on positive feelings from the moment your mind awakens. Smile within yourself with gratitude, for five seconds and try to do some of the exercises given in chapter 9. Make sure that you start your day on a thankful note by counting ten blessings about your life every morning. Thank God while feeling positive and keep smiling for a few seconds in silence, to help in release of positive hormones in the body. You will feel more positive about your life just by changing these mental vibrations, even if everything else remains the same, externally.

Though you may be engrossed in several different activities through the day, your inner axis remains set on the one feeling with which you start your day, which is called your point of INTERNAL DOMINANT

FOCUS. This IDF may shift to two or three feelings in a day though most people remain concentrated on one feeling of contentment or deprivation, through the day. Overtime, as you persistently focus on one feeling over others, your circumstances reflect the inner change that you create vibrationally.

For example, you can test that a persistent focus on feeling that you are in peace, would put you in a situation where you feel internally peaceful even in the midst of chaos. Similarly, a consistent focus on feeling that there is no peace, puts you often, in situations where you feel anxious and restless.

Likewise, a feeling that you are happily eating healthy food, would soon put you in a situation where you would be eating healthy food and feeling content. Similarly, a feeling that you do not have access to healthy food, would put you in situations where you feel deprived of good health.

From the soul's perspective as the co-creator, your future reality follows a cycle of complex manifestation of energies in physical form, created by focusing on a few dominant feelings over others. Feelings create ripples of vibrations in energy circuits which multiply to create physical forms and experiences over a period of time. The soul is the co-creator of its own reality and incarnates on Earth to understand the process of creation, as a co- creator. Metaphorically, if we imagine the Creator as a vast energy force like the SUN, each soul in a body is like ray of light which is a part of the Creator. Reality is created by spreading positive consciousness over nothingness. Feelings convert into form through the energy movement of the soul's focus in some directions over others. The more you focus on a feeling, the more you would emit energies towards manifesting it physically in your life.

Thus, by the same logic extended , the more you focus on your problems or the problems of the unhappy in the world, the more you increase difficulties and suffering ; and the more you focus on feeling positive about life, the more you increase emergence of abundance and being happy in the future.

In technical terms, creation of feelings of happiness in the future depends more on the internal vibrational focus than on action taken in the real world. Whether you can take action to solve a problem immediately or not , the more you focus on NOT HAVING, the more you energize the situations where you would feel deprived in the future; whereas the more you focus on HAVING, the more you create situations where you feel abundance in the future.

Vibrationally, a problem needs to be focused upon only as much as you can resolve it by your action, and detached from where it cannot be solved so that the internal dominant focus emits more positive energy than negative, on an average.

For example, the more fat you feel, the more you will indulge in over-eating ; whereas the more content you feel with your body, the more your internal mind will reset frequencies so that you continue feeling content and not fat . Irrespective of the dieting or exercise done by you to reduce fat, your feelings of being balanced affect your body weight more than the diet or exercise undertaken. Hence, to feel good about yourself, you have to work on resetting your inner emotional axis to deliberately feeling content so that your choices change overtime, from an inner urge to be balanced.

For the soul, the experience of being thin or fat; poor or rich are just manifestations of energy cycles which the mind is focused upon subconsciously. While your monetary income or beauty may improve by taking action in the real world to feel better, **your happiness would rise only when you choose to raise yourself from the cycle of deprivation to a cycle of contentment, with awareness of your feelings.**

(For example, the more starved you feel with the belief that you eat less, the more trapped you will be in energy cycles of weakness, deprivation of good food and helplessness over mal-nutrition. On the opposite side, the more obese you feel, the more trapped you will find yourself in cycles of indigestion, deprivation of feeling good and helplessness to self -control. The difference between negative frequencies of energies of starvation and obesity are small at energy levels as the energies of deprivation and helplessness are felt in both cases.)

From the energy/ soul manifestation perspective, negative feelings would manifest in any form if you continue to focus on negative vibrations. However, instead, if you practice focus on feeling contentment, and happiness, your routine vibration would create ripples of energy movement which would find/create several circumstances where you feel happy and content. But if you allow yourself to slip back towards sadness, when your routine focus is on '*what is missing*'; you, choose to reverse the vibration which would create happiness.

By the Laws of Soul Vibrations, happiness and peace increase by a constant, persistent focus on feeling happy, meaningful and peaceful; and not by a focus on fear, worry and anxiety of losing.

In the competitive world, children are constantly asked to work mechanically and promised that they would find happiness in adult lives. However, when they become adults, they realize that 'the promised happiness has not arrived automatically by being successful'. If the dominant focus from childhood is on taking action to be successful, at the cost of sacrificing idle time, peace and relaxation, there is no ease or peace in life, realized ever, at individual or mass levels.

Meditation helps in improving concentration and performance as the time on being peacefully idle helps rejuvenate the body's sense organs for performance mechanisms. The child needs to be trained to sit peacefully idle and put the sense organs at rest for rejuvenation by closing eyes and just feeling the breath of being alive. Being silent from all negative thinking for even a few seconds at intervals, helps to detach from routine worries and uplift the emotional energy circuits from negative to neutral.

Letting go of needing to perform is a mental exercise which helps the body's energies float up above anxiety. Rising above negative thinking energy circuits in the mind helps improve quality more than drowning in problems. Solutions to problems arise when the mind uplifts to a positive energy cycle, just as swimming is possible only after the child learns to float in idle waters.

Since, restless young minds are not trained in peacefulness, a struggle for success which begins in childhood never ends and happiness always appears far away, however old you become.

The mind gets conditioned into a habit of *doing* over *being*, and the person keeps drifting all the time towards more restless states of trying to find peace through increasing external pleasures, which is impossible.

Peace can be realized only by making internal choices to be peaceful.

The energy cycle of automatic negative thinking, once activated , cannot end unless the dominant internal focus is shifted to be silently content by choice to be positive, instead of seeking diversions like television/ alcoholism/ drugs/ food/ shopping/sports/ dancing etc. Instead of training the mind to keep worrying about *what is missing*, happiness is created by training the mind to be grateful for all that is, peaceful, detached and optimistic.

However, due to a deliberate habit of worrying activated by a mind training given to seek more improvement, there is never any contentment realized as the adult in the modern world remains restless, stressed and anxious by habit, guilt or choice.

Almost every person in the Modern World keeps pursuing happiness like searching for water in a desert and the craving continues, but the thirst never dissolves, as the water found is negligible, which creates a never ending chain of dissatisfaction.

The need for quenching inner thirst can be satiated by activating a deliberate release of positive hormones by focusing on being satisfied, from the beginning and creating more for further rejuvenation, and not out of deprivation. Metaphorically, if you feel satisfied with what you cook , you would still need to cook again for the next meal but you would cook better after taking a break for being content and rejuvenating the sense organs by sitting in peaceful states. But, if you keep working non-stop, your performance would fall due to not allowing positive fueling of the body through rest and relaxation. However, instead of allowing contentment to sink in for relaxation, the habit of remaining dis-satisfied by searching for *'what to do', all the time,* is drilled during schooling years as a motivational training for the mind.

As a result, there is a continuous release of negative hormones created by stress and no attention is given towards being in good health and developing satisfaction or contentment, which are necessary for releasing positive hormones. If you fall sick and heal and then again fall sick, you have to ensure that the body gets more healing space than being in the "falling sick" space, to remain in a positive soul frequency. But if you only release negative hormones without allowing the release of positive thinking and healthy hormones, you find yourself in constant states of bad health along with mental dis-satisfaction which inevitably leads to chronic/fatal diseases where negative hormones take over the body as the dominating energy.

After every next exam and after every successful result, there is always another exam to be prepared for and another sacrifice demanded. Happiness keeps getting postponed to the next victory; just as historically, happiness kept getting postponed to the next war.

Inner disappointment leads to violence outside though the intention of terrorism or wars is always to establish peace.

However, fighting for peace never leads to achievement of peace. History proves that emotional welfare of the common people did not rise by achieving victories in war. *The same emotional problems continue to rule human minds as they did when King Alexander, Julius Caesar, Maharaja Ashoka, Marie Antoinette , Napoleon or Jhansi ki Rani Lakshmi Bai were alive. Centuries changed but the negatively tilted emotional thought process did not evolve to positive. Crude violence reduced but consciousness did not uplift to as happier a state of being, as technology did. People continued to make the same emotional mistakes; manipulate, cheat and kill for success but never realized the happiness sought.*

Evidence has proved that this lop-sided approach of education which leads to blind pursuit of money and success has not led to happiness. Pursuit of marks in childhood leads to pursuit of money in adulthood and the cycle of compromise on peace continues by habit.

Making success a goal of life has been an automatic carryover of the mind-set of the survival instinct pursued by animals but it has acted as a blindly taken over thinking pattern, as discussed above.

Animals are simple in brain structure and are happy by getting food, sex and shelter. Each time an animal eats, it attains contentment .However, the need for human happiness incorporates needs for food with creativity, love with sex, compatibility with security, clothing with fashion, a variety of artefacts, wines and cuisines, educational development and satisfaction of all emotional desires which education creates .

Complex emotional experiences, traumas, sorrows, marriages and divorces are human and not animal like experiences. **Human happiness is a far more complex phenomenon than animal happiness and requires a far deeper understanding of the laws of existence, than an animal mind-set of fighting for survival, can satisfy.**

Creating dramatic suffering experiences or intensifying passionate happiness is an attribute of being distinctly human .Just teaching children to work on external factors to be happy makes them survival oriented and basic in thinking wherein they are unable to handle complex emotional problems which human satisfaction demands.

Emotional training cannot be sidelined for further human development as emotions cannot be killed. Emotional experiences help human beings feel alive and negating emotions kills the zeal to be happy. The soul in a human body co-creates life by focusing on some emotions over others.

There is a need for teaching children the Laws of Soul Vibrations in the universe and integrating these concepts in daily schooling. The laws of spirituality can be very easily applied with the regular education curriculum to bring patience in attitudes and meaningfulness in education.

Chapter 4 – The LAW OF CREATION

Integrating spirituality in education means spreading the awareness that each soul is a co-creator and creates its own reality by feeling specific vibrations while participating in collective creation of a world reality. The responsibility of education is to ensure that each soul concentrates on feeling positive/happy by choice and hence, energizes creation of happiness and not destruction of happiness.

Feelings create reality more than actions. Reality is perceived by the soul through feelings underlying experiences; be it happiness, success, misfortune or disease.

Feelings release electric impulses which create vibrationary movement in the direction which the feelings focus upon. Reality is co-created by each person (man, woman or child) by focusing on the vibrational movement of energy along a specific emotional path/ circuit.

A happy or positive or peaceful state of mind is a result of focusing on feelings of optimism, patience and peacefulness as deliberate choices of *being,* irrespective of what you are *doing.* (In case, you are constantly running a race, you need to create moments of peacefulness at regular intervals, as will be elaborated in the exercises given from chapter 8 onwards.)

Vibrations are released sub-consciously through the small electric impulses radiated underneath each feeling. These electric impulses release hormones in the body. Positive feelings generate positive/ happiness hormones in the body while negative hormones generate negative/stress hormones in the body.

Positive hormones improve health while negative hormones create sickness. For example, problems like asthma, headaches, colds and coughs are aggravated by continuously fueling the energy of feeling compromised (negatively pressurized, in conflict and suffocated, respectively) due to a choice to focus on negative circumstances of life.

Good Health and happiness are created by a deliberate choice of fueling an **internal dominant focus** on detached or positive feelings. Over a period of time, the consistent release of neutral or positive hormones helps you make choices of eating, exercising, thinking and meditating which heal the body and allow the mind to be free of overwhelming stress.

The most dominant feelings which are focused upon manifest as real situations, by activating changes in circumstances. It may take weeks, months or years for a new reality to manifest but a deliberate creation of imagining happiness in your future is better than leaving happiness to chance through depending on a trial and error process; because if you do not use your energies for mentally imagining happiness or creating inner peacefulness, you automatically invest your energies on fueling worries, sickness and stress.

While my other books viz. *"Creation Of Happiness: the Energy war, a Soul's Perspective "*, *"How To Be happy In Difficulties "* and *"A Course in Emotional Management"* ,
focus on explaining these vibratory concepts for adults, for improvements in health and peace of mind; the focus of this book is to teach how to apply the laws of vibration in everyday thinking from childhood. Hence, the three main laws of Vibration are simply explained in brief, in this book.

There are three main Laws of Soul Vibration which affect the vibrational movement of energy and creation of any reality in human life.

These three laws are

THE LAW OF CREATION

THE LAW OF REPETITION

THE LAW OF ATTRACTION

THE LAW OF CREATION

The Law of Creation states that you will create every feeling in your life which you focus upon by default.

By default means that your experiences will verify your internal dominant feelings whether your focus is intentional or non-intentional v. An intentional focus is where the person has an awareness of the impact of his thinking on his future. An awareness of inner focus is created by observation of the feelings one chooses to focus upon and a positive future is created by focusing on positive feelings which can be visualized in imagination.

A focus is non-intentional when we focus on a feeling subconsciously or feel depressed without an awareness that this focus will create more of the same feelings in the future. A routine focus is normally downward sloping or negative, as a downward sloping frequency is gravitationally automatic.

At a subconscious level, the more you focus on a feeling, the more you will radiate energies towards its manifestation in your life. For example, if you focus on the feeling that you are sad, all your circumstances would change to create more of this feeling of sadness. Your future circumstances would manifest such that the energy of sadness increases. Overtime, you will be in a circuit of sadness, wherein, the more you focus on the feeling that you are sad, the more your problems would increase so that you continue feeling sad.

The LAW OF CREATION operates automatically and governs all experiences of life.

For example, your LIKES and DISLIKES are governed by the LAW OF CREATION and change only when your internal focus changes to another feeling of *likes or dislikes* by choice, new awareness or by shock. For example, you may love eating meat till you develop severe indigestion and have to start disliking your choice. However, if you do not change your choice, indigestion would become a part of your life.

In absence of a different choice, your circumstances keep adjusting in alignment with your dominant choice of feelings and the same choices continue to rule your life even while external circumstances keep changing. Often, the choice is between greed and good health or materialism and peace of mind.

For instance, if you get indigestion by eating non-vegetarian food and choose to stay in good health instead of choosing for taste, you may shift to vegetarian food and feel happy while eating; overtime, your circumstances would be created so that you enjoy eating vegetarian food.

Similarly, your vibrational preferences decide your routine. For example, if you feel that you like dancing, you would co-create opportunities to dance. You may watch television programs on dance, get good dance teachers, have friends who like dance, dance in functions and parties etc. However, if you focus on the feeling that you do not like dancing, you will opt out of dancing programs in school, prefer watching other programs on television and stay away from people who like dancing.

Similarly, if you think that you like studying, you would take interest in academics, invest time on studying, feel happy with getting new knowledge etc. However, if you dislike studying, you would avoid investing your time and effort on academics .The more you choose to dislike academics, the more your circumstances would automatically get designed such that you can comfortably dislike studying more as you grow up. You may get a non-conducive, non-academic home environment, a non – understanding school curriculum and/or you may have friends who dislike studies.

In effect, every feeling which you voluntarily and automatically dwell upon will co-create the reality of your life, by your own subconscious choice, irrespective of the actions you do on the basis of the preaching of others, your own self-talk, ambitions or desires.

The feeling which you think about the most is called the point of INTERNAL DOMINANT FOCUS. This feeling sends out the maximum energy of manifestation. For example, you may tell yourself that you want to be slim and content, but keep focusing on feelings of discontent/ deprivation in your life. Feelings of discontentment will motivate you to find short-term contentment, which would motivate you eat more and become fat.

Similarly, you may focus upon the feeling that you want to do well in academics but also, keep focusing on the feeling that you find studies meaningless to your current circumstances. That will prevent you from studying as your feelings will take you towards activities which you find more meaningful to your current situation.

Likewise, you may keep telling yourself that you want to perform well in sports but keep feeling that you do not like running meaninglessly for applause. Again, as long as you do not like the feeling involved, you would not play well in sports, however much you believe that you should.

There can be several reasons for not performing as ambitions dictate. You may get scolded for not performing well but your soul/ subconscious mind would only create the feelings which align with your inner truth. Your subconscious energies will move along with your feelings/ electric impulses and will not motivate your body to move along with your self-enforced desires which would be based on general thinking or mass consciousness beliefs. The default feelings which you focus involuntarily upon will manifest whether your conscious, rational mind agrees or not.

The laws of vibration ensure that you manifest feelings which you like to think about repeatedly, whether negative or positive, and not your words or thoughts or desires, unless they make an impact in your subconscious which is so deep that it makes you change your inner focus of dominant feelings and hence, vibrationary energy cycles.

The following exercise and all exercises in further chapters are simple in application but may appear difficult while reading, just as cycling would appear difficult if you read about it, until you apply and practice the techniques read.

Practical Exercise 2 (PE 4.1) – Co-creation of Reality

Practice focusing deliberately on two simple imagined feelings till your focus becomes natural and feels real

To start learning deliberate co-creation of reality, choose to focus upon one simple positive feeling and one simple negative feeling.

For example, for creating a positive feeling - you can focus on the feeling that you are eating *carrot/ice-cream/ anything else which you like* and feel happy about it.

Concept: Feeling happy while eating is the key positive vibration to focus upon, in this imaginative exercise. The intention is to increase positive hormones by feeling good with every activity undertaken, so that accumulative happiness rises in the *being* .The same exercise can be transferred to any activity like playing a game as a child or having a sexual experience as an adult; wherein the happiness which you seek from your action will be created mentally in imagination before the activity manifests.

The idea is to plan the feeling of the outcome desired instead of planning the action desired; so that circumstances manifest to get the desired feeling and actions change accordingly, if needed, so that happiness manifests as a necessary outcome and is not left to trial and error. We are essentially, shifting the paradigm of the mind, from success as the goal of an experience,   to obtaining a positive frequency/ happiness from success, as the goal.

Activity:
In your imagination - activate all your sense organs for creating the desired feeling. See yourself eating the carrot/ice-cream/anything else. See the imagined ice-cream. Taste the imagined ice-cream. Smell the imagined ice-cream. Touch the imagined ice-cream with a spoon, hear the sounds in your mouth and around just as you would while eating and activate your sense organs deliberately as they would automatically activate in the real experience. Also, focus on the feeling of contentment after eating the ice-cream. A good feeling and positive hormonal discharge will get created as an outcome of the activation of your sense organs. Focus on this nice feeling several times in a day to keep creating positive vibrations but do not allow yourself to dip into focusing on negative vibrations simultaneously, as much as possible. .

TEST YOURSELF – If you have focused accurately by activating all your sense organs, the nice feeling will come true in your life in reality sooner or later. Whether you literally eat ice-cream or not, this feeling will suddenly come true through some pleasant experience on the same day or in the next few days. Some people may actually be led to eat the ice-cream while others may get the same positive experience through eating something else. The positive feeling may even manifest through you feeling an urge and going to buy an ice-cream.

Similarly, for creating a negative feeling - you can focus on the feeling that you are eating a vegetable and feeling bad about it. Involve all your sense organs on creating the negative feeling just as you create worries. Imagine the clumsy look of the vegetable, smell the irregular odor, touch the sogginess, feel the sour or bitter taste, hear the compromising thoughts when you have to eat the vegetables and feel negative.   Focus on the negative feeling of compromise/sadness several times a day or till the experience manifests. Your positive frequency will fall as your focus on negative frequency rises. Whether you eat the vegetable or not, the low frequency negative feeling will manifest in some way in your experience within the next few hours or days and you would feel sad/ unhealthy as with a spirit of low frequency.

Simple exercises pave the way for complicated exercises on positive thinking .Keep testing till you realize that you are manifesting the feelings which you have previously dwelled upon, automatically.

Testing yourself is easy if you do not feel reverse feelings, during initial practice. For example, in case, you manifest the opposite feelings viz. that you felt sick after eating the ice-cream and relaxed after eating the vegetable , it would happen because you focused on the opposite feeling involuntarily while thinking rationally that you are focusing on the straight feeling. In case you manifest reverse feelings, manifestation would reverse. For example, an evolved or old soul would naturally find ice-creams unhealthy to eat and vegetables tasty without any preaching needed to create the effect and hence would feel negative in the experiences society labels as happy.

It is only the feelings which are subconsciously fueled that manifest, and not the feelings conventionally desired. The ambitions, advice, words of self-talk or good thoughts which you focus upon will not manifest directly, unless they are accompanied by positive feelings.

Thus, if you manifest opposite feelings, it would be a clue that your feelings are opposite to your self talk and you need to concentrate more on your inner self to find your true beliefs. However, if your feelings manifest as you visualize in your mind, it is a clue that your words and feelings match and your inner self is aligned with your rational belief.

By practicing this exercise and similar exercises, you will surely start manifesting simple desires, as soon as you stop believing that it cannot happen. Delay in manifestation is created by resisting the outcome. The Laws of Vibrations always come true. As you persistently practice, the feelings which you focus upon will manifest and you will realize how you automatically create reality through your internal dominant focus.

Practical exercise 3 (PE 4.2): Co-creation of desired emotional experiences

Focus on imagined emotional experiences instead of the above mentioned physical experiences and observe how your imagined feelings create happiness and sadness in your life in the near future.

Examples of emotional feelings which you can focus upon –

For a positive feeling, you may imagine feeling applauded by a teacher/parent for doing some good work or a friend happily playing with you. Key vibration to be imagined is *a feeling of happiness* whatever the scenario is.

Activate all your sense organs in the imagination as they would when you literally feel happy. Imagine the classroom or house scenario where you are applauded, hear the glee in the voice of the teachers, touch your skin as it expands to absorb the positive energy as you hear the words, taste your mouth as it wants to take in the soothing feeling of the words being spoken in your praise, smell the familiar pleasant air and feel the happiness in the situation as you would if it were happening in real. If you activate the sense organs accurately, you would feel praised in a similar manner (probably in smaller or bigger intensity) in a few hours or days. As you keep focusing on the feelings of being praised, the intensity of happiness would rise and you would be more praised in the future.

For a negative feeling, you may imagine feeling sad because of being scolded by a teacher/parent or a friend fighting with you. Hear the sadness in the parent/teacher's voice, see the angry /hurt expression , touch your skin as it recoils to resist being scolded, taste your mouth as it wants to spit out the energy of abuse, smell the disharmony in the air and feel the unhappiness rising in you . This scenario will manifest abuse and disharmony in your life shortly after you manifest it in your imagination.

Once you are aware that you can create the feelings you focus upon, cut yourself from the negative situation mentally as soon as possible and erase the memory with white paint rubber in your mind as if erasing a painting on a paper. This is a brief outline of the technique of erasing memories which ensures that the energy of negative frequency gets dissipated in the subconscious mind and an automatic memory of sadness does not perpetuate. Replace the memory of the sad film in your mind with creating a happy film in your imagination in the same space and feeling happy as the last, lingering vibration. The change in inner vibrational focus will activate a change in your external circumstances again and you will be able to feel happy.

Precaution - Be careful about the negative feelings you choose; and when sadness comes in as reality, be aware that you have created the reality with your own inner focus of fearing the worst. Negative feelings manifest faster than positive feelings as sloping down is easier than uplifting yourself. Fear and abuse stay on in mind as there is magnetic energy in negative frequencies; whereas positive feelings have higher frequencies which make you fly in happiness with increasing optimism and faith but require an uphill climb/deliberate choice to be sustained mentally. (Molecules of negative feelings are dense and magnetic while molecules of positive feelings are freer, less magnetic and more spaced out. That is why sadness comes fast but happiness takes a sustained vibration to stay on. Negative energy has tension which binds you while positive energy has detachment which generates freedom. These concepts are explained in some more detail in my book *Creation Of happiness: the Energy War, a soul's perspective)*

The LAW OF CREATION operates by default whether you deliberately choose to focus on a specific feeling or not. If you do not direct your focus towards a specifically desired feeling, the law of creations operate to create the feelings which you normally focus upon.

When you feel that you are unhappy, it implies that your normal focus is negative and it would help you rise to a happier state of *being* by upgrading your internal dominant focus to more positive, through applying the techniques given, as you read on.

Chapter 5 – Factors Influencing the Law of Creation

The purpose of enhancing thinking ability is to co-create a happy world by having the awareness that positive thinking is a choice of uplifting the self, unlike negative thinking which gets automatically activated by gravitating towards a focus of sliding down with energies of deprivation.

The Law of Creation works each and every time at a vibrational energy level. Everything that exists in the physical world has an energy hologram attached to it. Till an energy blue print is created, nothing can manifest in the physical world. The Law of Creation is subconsciously applied to create any real experience in the physical world or to destroy a previously created unpleasant experience.

The reason why the Law of Creation has not yet spread scientifically is that it is difficult to prove it exists in the physical dimension by depending on purely tangible evidence. The Law of Creation activates energy cycles from the subconscious mind, which can be tested through accessing vibrations of feelings but cannot be tested by physical proofs.

> Physical proof of any phenomenon is created by activation of sense organs. The human being connects to the world through his/her sense organs. You believe something exists if you can see it, hear it, touch it, smell it or taste it. The five sense organs viz. eyes, ears, nose, tongue and skin are transmitters which create sensations in the body. Physical evidence depends on perception of solids/liquids by the sense organs whereas the Law of Creation can only be felt as energy movement, of air with a positive or negative vibration.

You cannot see energy movement or hear or touch it or taste it or smell it. However, you can feel the energy moving through feeling sensations of pleasure or dis-pleasure. Energy movements create sensations which are electric impulses. These electric impulses release hormones that are felt as positive feelings or negative feelings.

Positive sensations release positive feelings in the energy fields of the body while unpleasant sensations create negative feelings /negative electric impulses. Positive feelings generate positive hormones in the body which improve health, joy, optimism and mental capacities. Negative feelings generate negative hormones in the body which create stress, bad health and negative expectations from life.

reality appears to be ruled by your Your external circumstances because you are not aware that you are being led to co-create your own circumstances by your inner focus on some energies as prioritized feelings over others.

When the sense organs generate feelings, energy is released in the body which is received by the soul as a vibrational movement. Positive feelings charge the soul battery with positive electric impulses and increase the soul's positive vibrational frequency, thus improving its good health & brightness; while negative feelings generate negative electric impulses which reduce the soul's power, lower its vibrational frequency and create sickness & helplessness.

In essence, your soul is the co-creator of the reality which you encounter in your life. The soul is a fragment of the spirit of God which you may refer to as *Life force / Creator* in the human body. This spirit is, metaphorically, a unit of electric life force like the filament of a bulb that is connected to a higher unit of life force. The human spirit takes in a unit of life force energy from the Higher Self, to spread it as its consciousness manifesting expressively on the physical realm of Earth. However, the spirit perceives only electric impulses which are the sensations created in response to feelings.

Reality for the soul is an illusion, literally, as it exists as an experience of feelings and is co-created only as a vibrationary manifestation of the energy of internal dominant focus. External forms manifest as internal energies of creation complexifies into physical forms and variation is perceived   through feeling different intensities underlying different physical experiences.

Every feeling releases positive or negative electric impulses, depending on information taken in by the sense organs. These positive or negative electric impulses are read as experiences of life by the spirit on Earth.

Feelings are released when sense organs receive information and generate an electric impulse in the subconscious mind.   Each sense organ generates a signal/electric impulse which releases a feeling in the body. For example, when you eat, you use the sense organ of taste which creates a pleasant or unpleasant sensation in you that leads to creation of a positive or negative feeling. Similarly, the sense organs of sound create pleasant or unpleasant sensations while hearing external sounds which generate positive or negative feelings in the inner self. Likewise, the sense organs of eyes, nose and skin create pleasant or unpleasant feelings associated with visons, smell and touch. All five sense organs are useful for the body as they combine sensory experiences which create feelings in the body.

Creation happens by focusing on information which matches your dominating energy movement in the subconscious mind. The body is your machine of creation which helps you decide on where to focus and channel energies, just as a torch is used to focus light. Like components of a machine, your sense organs have limited capacity to take in information from the world and convert it into electric signals. Hence, your sense organs assign focus depending on your internal priorities. Thus, there are several bits of information which are not absorbed by the sense organs because they are focusing on something else, as current priority.

For example, if you are focusing on a song playing inside your mind, you may not hear the words of your teacher. Similarly, as an adult, if you focus more on the exterior packaging than on the quality of a product, you may ignore some good products which are not as well packaged and instead, buy some inferior products.

As is explained in my book "*A Course In Emotional Management* ", it has been researched that out of 2.3 million bits of information, only 7 +- 2 bits of information are perceived by the brain as truth. Remaining bits of information are rejected as irrelevant. That is why different students learn differently because each focuses on different bits of information from the same syllabus taught.

Your subconscious mind and the soul are pure energy units and only perceive energies as different intensities of experiences. Future reality is co-created on the basis of the present internal dominant focus.

For example, if you are hugged by a friend, you may have a positive feeling vibration in the body. However, your soul would only feel the vibration and not the physical hug. If you imagine the hug instead of it actually happening, the soul would still feel almost as positive. Also, if you imagine that you would be hugged in the future, your soul would start recording and co-creating positive vibrations. Similarly, if a parent slaps you, your soul would record the vibration and not the physical slap. If your parent scolds you harshly, you may feel as negative as through a physical slap. Also, if you worry that you will be slapped in the future, your soul would start recording and co-creating negative vibrations.

Therefore, your feelings are an indication of the reality which you are creating in your future. The present emotions which you focus upon dominantly will shape the emotions which you will experience as your life moves on. If you can guide your internal dominant focus by practice to remain neutral or positive, your future emotional experiences would be non negative or positive, irrespective of your success in the external world. But if you allow fear, stress and anxiety to rule over your sensibilities, you would lose track of happiness while running the rat race.

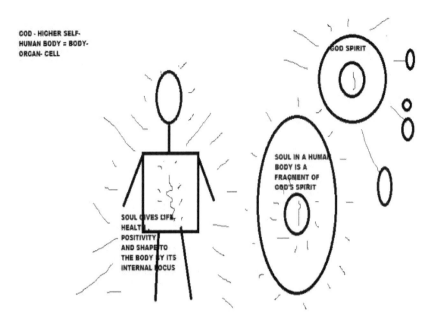

GOD - HIGHER SELF-
HUMAN BODY = BODY-
ORGAN- CELL

GOD SPIRIT

SOUL IN A HUMAN
BODY IS A
FRAGMENT OF
GOD'S SPIRIT

SOUL GIVES LIFE,
HEALTH,
POSITIVITY
AND SHAPE TO
THE BODY BY ITS
INTERNAL FOCUS

The Law of Creation has to be tested as an energy vibration and applied with practice to create happiness & contentment in your life, which you always desire to achieve by your efforts to be successful. Your happiness and positive vibrations are measured as success, by your soul. Happiness does not rise as an internal dominant focus by depending on external measures of positivity such as getting good marks, high grades, good money or luxuries. Due to the limited focusing capacity of the human brain, you cannot disregard a phenomenon just because proof does not exist in tangible/physical terms.

For example, dogs can see only black and white but that does not mean that other colors do not exist. Similarly, snakes see only red, elephants hear sounds which human beings cannot hear and everyone feels God's presence. Those who depend on sensory evidence, reject God's presence as illusory and thereby, disconnect from receiving positive vibrations from a higher unit of Life Force. A bulb disconnected from its generator cannot radiate light. Similarly, a human being disconnected from God does not feel happy or vibrant about life and overtime, there are extreme feelings of loneliness, bad health & bitterness experienced in people who refuse to believe God exists simply because they cannot see God.

((

Note -

Scientifically, God cannot be seen ever as God is an energy of a very high frequency and cannot be condensed in a physical, dense form and hence,   is never seen or heard, physically, by using human sense organs. Just as an ant cannot claim to see a human being fully, or a bulb cannot see the generator; a physical body cannot see God, literally. Those who claim to see God access apparitions or projections or energy holograms. The Gods which have incarnated in physical forms have been historically subjected to human karmic limitations and have had to suffer positive energy loss by negative thinking as part of karmic suffering.

The Cosmic energy of God exists for those who believe in the spiritual self as receptivity of energies is through accessing thought waves. You receive the frequencies of thought waves which you already believe in as creation is a manifestation of internal dominant focus governed by the mind...

Since movement of energy is vibrational, if you do not believe, you will not find God till you start entering the realm of belief.

Though people like to worship God in form, the energy of God exists as a cosmic force. You would connect to God if you believe but not if you just worship an idol or read a scripture without belief.

God vibrates units of positive life force energy which feel your soul and connect to you through vibrational matching of positive energy frequencies, during moments of inner silence where your own feelings are neutral or positive in frequency. You perceive God's positive energies when you are not negative, restless or agitated. The rays of God enter through your inner space as energy of positive strength during moments of peace generated in meditation/silencing the mind, chanting of prayers to generate positive feelings, or while feeling positive vibrationally through experiences of happiness, gratitude, good health, feeling loved and optimism

God does not directly hear prayers or mantras but can feel the vibrations underlying positively felt chanting and connects to the body at a vibrational dimension. The Higher Spirit can only perceive your feelings underlying your prayers and not the words or rituals For example, you may not connect to God if you light a lamp or say a prayer mechanically but you will connect to God if you do the same action with positive feelings involved...

God, as the ultimate positive life force, is a spirit and does not have a body which has physical sense organs. If you ask God to solve all your problems, you would also have to feel like a spirit without a body and dissolve the negative energy of your problems by focusing positive energy of light on the negative density of difficulties. From the perspective of the soul, the difficulties encountered in a human body are like rocks to be broken by focusing positive life force consciousness in the course of learning evolution.

If you feel good while praying, God receives positive radiation from you and you receive life force energy/ healing/ intuitions/ guidance as transmissions into the body's energy circuits from cosmic light. Hence, when you pray with faith that you will receive; the cosmic light sends back positive vibrations of matching frequencies.

God does not receive negative vibrations as God is a purely positive vibrational force of energy. When you feel negative and pray, your problems rise overtime by the vibratory LAW OF CREATION as you start producing negative electric impulses by worrying.

The human body can never be completely positive and hence, a spirit in a human body would always be subjected to some negative dense energy, which holds it in a physical form. The negative energy of the soul has to be regularly cleansed from extra negative thoughts (past memories of sadness/ traditional redundant beliefs etc.) just as a mobile phone or laptop needs cleansing from extra debris. The cleansing can be done by mental exercises on feeling positive, dissolving worries, self-healing and taking energy showers of positive cosmic light - given in the exercises from chapters 9 onwards, which aim to erase your focus on negative feelings and redirect focus to feeling positive.

Your training needs to be such that you can directly connect to God through your own Higher Spirit and seek help through activating a positive vibrational energy transfer.

If you seek a guru or evidence that God exists, the free spirit of God may connect to you by entering in a physical form, as in a saint ; but whether the body of the Guru channels God or not , would depend on how you feel while seeing the person or hearing the messages. If the energy transferred is positive, the physical person would be radiating God's consciousness. However, the same person may become negative and not channel God's energies at different moments. If the energy transferred is confused or negative, the person may not be a clear channel of God. Not all bodies which speak as channels of God on Earth are clear of debris or negative thinking.))

The subconscious mind co-creates reality through feeling it. Hence, if you can test how your feelings are creating your current reality over a period of time, you would realize that the Law of Creation manifests your reality in the same direction as your present feelings are moving, in the future. You would know whether you have created a reality or not by the way you feel, whether the phenomenon can be verified by external sensory evidence or not. You always create feelings in the future in alignment with how you feel in the present situation.

Since the dominant feelings which you focus upon

manifest automatically, it is wise to be aware of the feelings which you choose to focus upon so that you have control over your future rather than feel helpless. Using the Law of Creation with awareness helps in gaining control of your life and circumstances such that you can feel happy with the efforts you desire. Allowing the Law of Creation to work without awareness usually results in manifestation of desires without accompanying happiness.

Whether you choose to be aware of your routine feelings or not, the Law of Creation would act on your vibrations by default. However, if you choose to focus on feeling happy with awareness, you would direct your reality towards increasing happiness in the future.

Chapter 6 - Testing and Applying the Law of Creation

*Fantasize and co-create a reality which aids in Creation Of happiness in your Life where you manifest good health, abundance, passion, creativity, optimism, love and peace, by deliberate visualized focus. For, if you fuel worrying about success without balancing your inner peace, you may **co**-create a reality which leads to destruction of happiness, good health & harmony.*

Our education system focuses on success but not on happiness. However, if success does not lead to increasing happiness, good health, optimism and peace, it automatically increases energies of distress, unrest, anxiety and bad health. To manifest happiness with success, children need to be trained in using the Law of Creation from primary years of education.

The following factors need to be considered while implementing the LAW OF CREATION with awareness in daily life with choice.

1. The Law of Creation converts thoughts & energies (radiating from the electric impulses released from your feelings) into real physical experiences over a period of time. Conversion of energy into form takes time to manifest.

2. The Law of Creation can only be tested by feeling sensations/energies underlying experiences. There may be no physical proof available in short spans of time. Overtime, as technology manifests or circumstances change, persistent feelings may exactly manifest physically.

3. The Law of Creation can give unpredictable outcomes if there is mis-match between the feelings desired and thoughts/actions/ visuals / ambitions being focused upon.

4. The Law of Creation cannot be used to manifest desires of happiness which are not in alignment with your inner beliefs and values, as feelings/energies radiate subconsciously.

5. The Law of Creation works to create happiness only if you do not remain worried all the time and learn how to develop detachment to problems. Whenever you are sad/angry, your energy frequency is negative. Happiness is an energy of a positive vibrational frequency. Energy has to move to a zero/neutral state to become positive vibrationally, which happens when the problem is resolved or you detach from it.

6. The Law of Creation is not governed by ethics. The vibratory law will create negative and positive experiences automatically on the basis of the vibrations of the feelings which you focus upon, even if the negative manifestation is bad for you, rationally.

7. The Law of Creation operates at an energy level which is affected by other people's feelings focused upon the same reality, as in a matrix of vibrationary exchanges. Your feelings will be influenced by other people's thinking/vibrations and may manifest sooner or get destroyed by the impact of other people's energies dominating your feelings.

8. The Law of Creation will create circumstances on the basis of your dominant, chosen vibrations automatically; Happiness cannot be created just by your words or verbal commands. It has to be felt as an energy radiating from within. To create happiness, you have to make choices to feel happy and not just tell yourself that you want to be happy while feeling sad. Happiness is created only if small feelings of happiness are focused upon consistently. On the other hand, sadness is created, if continuous feelings of dissatisfaction/deprivation are focused upon, irrespective of success in the outside world

These features are briefly explained below:

Feature 1 - *The Law of Creation does not operate instantly. It may take hours/ days/ weeks/ years or centuries for the law of creation to manifest the feelings which the soul has been focusing upon.*

For example, the aero plane was visualized four hundred years before it actually flew. Similarly, every internal dominant focus manifests overtime. To illustrate, diseases in the human body take about seven years to manifest from the seed of a negative thought, like asthma starts with the feelings of being unfairly or unreasonably suppressed by authoritative members of the family; diabetes starts with feelings of self –blame and cancer starts with focusing on suppressed anger instead of releasing the emotional energy of helplessness.

Simple feelings manifest sooner than complex phenomenon which involve activation of desires in a group. For example, the feeling of eating an ice-cream/soup/anything you like, individually, if focused upon with keenness, may manifest literally, in real, within a day but the feeling of eating and having fun in a school picnic would take weeks to manifest, depending on the feelings desired by all other people involved.

You can use the Law of Creation to change yourself with far more ease than other people. That is because it is easier to change internal dominant focus of energies, within self than change vibrational mind-sets of others. If your desire involves changing vibrations of other people, it becomes a complex desire.

Where complex outcomes are desired, it is necessary to focus for long-term with concentration, perseverance and patience. Belief, detachment and optimism are also needed for the larger vibrations to manifest; with the ability to let go of negative thinking to build new patterns of soul vibrations. Long term desires of happiness necessitate an ability to change and to not get dissuaded with failure.

Practical exercise 4 (PE 6.1) – Test Manifestation

Focus on the feeling that you have the results/grades which you desire to have in your mid-term exams. Write down the statement on a sheet of paper or make a pseudo report card with the desired grades.

You may write any of the following statements on the paper:

"I have received grade "A "in all my exams, Thank You Soul /God "or
"I have been rewarded for my good performance. Thank you Soul/ God "or
"Thank you God that I feel successful, content and happy "
Or write any statement which would give you positive feelings in the long run

Then, stick this paper on the wall which you can see every night. Before sleeping, look at this imagined report card and feel that you have literally received the grades written on it. Feel the joy in your stomach that you have the desired grades. Say mentally "Thank You God that I have the desired grades and I am making every choice to manifest what I desire ".

As you keep repeating the affirmation to yourself with belief, your mind-set would change to be optimistic. In tune with this new mind-set, you would automatically, start making changes in your lifestyle, sleeping patterns and study habits such that the concentration with which you make efforts grows.

You may get your desire soon if your vibrations of positive belief match the outcome state. If you are very far behind your desire, it may take time for the desire to manifest. Initially, you may not get the exact grades which you desire but you will keep improving overtime, till you achieve specifically what your soul desires. You will find that your grades would start improving as you keep repeating this affirmation to yourself. You would also start making different choices of studying which help you acquire the desired grades. Your sleeping time may also increase as good sleep is necessary for better understanding of the subject, improves concentration and helps in relaxing the mind from stress as does meditation.

You can test that your manifestation is working by testing your feelings about the outcome desired. If belief is greater than doubt, it signals that the subconscious mind has accepted the manifestation and started working upon it. The energy would start growing within you with the realization that you need better grades. It may take a few weeks or months for changes to manifest on the physical plane as old habits would have to be discarded before new thinking patterns set in.

Feature 2 - *The Law of creation can be tested only at the level of feeling an* *experience. There may be no physical proof that the law of Creation is coming true in your life.*

You can use the Law of creation to become healthy if you are sick, to become slim if you are fat , to get a new job when you desire to work, to earn more money , to increase confidence , dance, sing, play , have new friends etc.

The technique of manifestation is the same as described above but mastery over doubts is necessary for the desired imagination, to become a reality, over a period of time wherein your focus needs to persistently remain on feeling optimistic. You can master doubts and negative thinking only by overcoming the energy within you which creates negative thinking.

Continuing on the above example, if you are focusing on the feeling that you are getting an A grade in an exam and feeling good that you have understood your subject well, the only clue that you are literally studying well, would be your feelings of improvements in concentration/understanding. It is not necessary that you will perform well in every short term test if you are aiming at an overall good understanding of the subject. Short term failure will create doubt in you which you will have to overcome by remaining persistently hopeful.

Secondly, visualizing a desire would help you understand whether you want to make the efforts to pursue the desire or you prefer giving up on it, thus freeing your mind from stress & conflict.

For example, if you are generally bad in studies, visualizing a good grade will not change your study habits overnight until your beliefs or attitude towards studies change. Your subconscious mind will not help you get a good grade if you feel sad or negative while studying as the soul energy will motivate you to vibrate towards a more positively, engaging vibration, as every soul desires a positive internal vibrational frequency to raise its power as the co-creator.

Thus, if you feel that you have no interest in studying, you can give up on your desire to have good grades, stop worrying, study only as needed for passing through a ritual and instead use your energy for excelling in another area in which you have interest.

Visualizing a good grade with feeling negative would make you lose interest in studying but help you find another area of interest where you can get good grades. However, visualizing a good grade in studies. With feeling positive would slowly motivate your subconscious mind to redirect your energies to study with interest & concentration.

The subconscious mind gives you signals that the Law of Creation is working when you feel more satisfied about yourself .Feelings take time to change direction from negative to positive but once the positive attitude is built up with a focus on feeling happy, it becomes a routine way of life. Small feelings of being successful with being happy, multiply your positive energy overtime.

Practical Exercise 5 (PE 6.2) - Applying 'Feel Good 'Affirmations

The technique of positive affirmations can be applied to all areas of life but it works only when you feel good while saying the affirmations to yourself. If you do not feel good but feel sad and talk positive, the soul records negative vibrations and the outcome co-created creates sadness in the long term, in spite of positive self talk or positive preaching or short-term positive results.

For example, you may be sick and you want to feel healthy again or you may be overweight and you want to feel slim & active.

You may start by repetitively telling yourself that you are healthy, with feeling/ visualizing the same scenario in imagination. Initially, positive imagination will hold only for moments as the inner negative thinking currents would be pre-dominating. The positive vibrations will stay longer if you keep shifting your mind-set to feel good by stopping your mind from worrying even if only for a few seconds, as repetitively as possible. All thoughts/ feelings repeat themselves and if you do not break currents of negativity and deliberately repeat feelings of positivity, your old negative feelings will restart ruling your habitual thinking.

While using words in self - talk/ affirmations, it is necessary to feel grateful, as the energy of gratitude multiplies the positive energies of receipt which you need to support your existence, while taking actions to succeed.

You may thank God, your soul, your body or any energy whose co-operation you seek to increase in your life.

You may use the following words:
"I like my own body and I make choices to feel healthy & active. Thank You, Life-force/God"
Or "Thank You God, my sickness is gone and I am healthy again "
Or "Thank You God I am eating, thinking and exercising so that I feel healthy, slim & active ".
Or "Thank you God, I am in control of my life, my eating habits, and my health and am achieving the energy vibration of who I desire to be"
Or any statement that you specifically desire to achieve …

Before sleeping at night, you can write and read this affirmation and feel as good about your body in your imagination. Feel the movement of being in a healthy body while saying the words as the feeling of being in good health, are the key to creation of reality. The emotions you feel before sleeping at night and repetitively during the day, go as instructional data to the subconscious mind. Overtime, you will find that you start making choices of eating, exercising, taking medicines and self- healing that help you acquire the body and health which you desire.

Visualizing/ affirming the desires to yourself, mentally, before taking action would ensure that you do not waste energy in worrying by focusing on fear & doubts. Also, clarity in your self -talk would help you choose the correct diet and the most suitable exercises for yourself, given your circumstances. Overtime, you would find that just by feeling good and telling yourself repetitively that you like your body, you will start rejecting foods, drugs and exercises which make you feel unhealthy .

Applying the Law of Creation and testing it to ensure that it is making you feel good with every day which passes by, would help you more than just taking advise externally from health professionals without giving any clear instruction on how you desire to feel, to your subconscious mind.

 Positive energies will increase in your life more by taking time out once a day for **writing** down ten desired feelings and thanking God, for helping you make the choices which help you feel happier about those spheres of your life where you are working to help yourself.

Feature 3 - *The Law of Creation gives unpredictable outcomes if the feelings or desires being focused upon are different from the intentions being focused upon.*

Every desire which you believe would get you happiness may not get you the contentment you have envisaged if your desire is a mirage. People in adult lives keep working to become financially successful while ignoring their inner needs for relaxation and freedom; but the money they earn fails to bring them the contentment they desire. Similarly, wars were fought in history for getting justice to the masses, but the victories did not lead to increase in mass welfare of the common people. People still suffer from the same traumas of injustice as they did hundreds of years back as money from the victories was not spent on developing emotional welfare but was wasted on opulence or establishing religious supremacy.

In everyday life, for example, if you desire a new friend or lover, your intention needs to be clear. If you desire respect from a lover, you need to find someone who would give you respect and not just coffee. If you accept less, there will be boredom and detachment from the friend and craving for respect from the same friend or another, will continue till you receive that energy which you sought originally.

The same logic which applies to complex phenomenon applies to Base experience. You would feel dissatisfied with an outcome if your *feeling desired- intention desired - action planned - expected outcome* are not in alignment with the originally desired positive frequency .

For example, you may be consistently desiring a new bag/toy/ car / house/ clothes/ friend/ love etc. and feeling deprived that you do not have what you crave for. Let us keep the metaphor desired as a *toy* which represents the energy that you seek to possess. As you grow older, the desire for a toy can convert into the desire for a real car or a lover but the base desire sets your vibrational thinking patterns. As a child, you may believe that you will be happy after you get the new toy. However, when the new toy comes in, you may not feel the complete satisfaction that you expected. You keep craving for more and remain dis-satisfied. This mis-match in desire and outcome happens because your dominant focus was on the feeling of being deprived of the toy; hence, the dominant focus of dis-satisfaction continues even when you have the toy, as an external reality is not perceived by the soul.

The subconscious mind would not record the happiness in your life which came in with the toy, unless you feel positive in your inner self when you have the toy and continue to focus on feeling grateful and content, internally. Your happiness will increase your positive soul frequency, confidence & concentration if you focus on the positive energy of satisfaction upon receiving what you desire, and do not allow your worries to dilute your happiness immediately there-after.

To manifest happiness with success, and get the desired feeling of satisfaction, you need to focus directly on the feeling of satisfaction and not on the dominant feeling of deprivation of not having.

From the perspective of mobilizing vibrations – "*I have/ want to have* … "is a higher positive vibration than "*I don't have and I want* …*"* If you focus on wanting without feeling negative, your dominant focus would move from neutral to positive automatically.

A direct focus on visualizing/imagining the feeling of satisfaction which you expect from the new toy or new car would lead you sooner to receive or buy what you desire. Also, by practicing feeling satisfied, you will choose the object which makes you feel happy and not invest on any toy/ clothes/ car which may not give you satisfaction later.

Very often, people buy things or enter relationships based on surface glitter which do not lead to internal satisfaction later because the focus is on the external product and not on the spirit of satisfaction. However, by focusing on inner satisfaction than on the external glitter, you would be intuitively led to choose a product which gets you satisfaction.

Also, even if you do not have any hope of receiving a new toy/car/love, a focus on the feeling that you have the car and satisfaction along with it, would automatically mobilize your circumstances such that the satisfaction manifests on an increasing indent.

Practical exercise 6 (PE 6.3) – Activation of Negative Feelings

Visualize something that you desire and feel deprived that you do not have it. Feel the tension. Wait for an hour/day. Observe the energy spreading.

Test yourself- Feelings of tension and unease in other areas of your life would indicate that you have focused on negative feelings in one area of life.

Practical Exercise 7 (PE 6.4) - Activation of Positive Feelings

Before focusing, deliberately connect Intention with Thought & Action. **Mentally imagine a sequence of Intended Feeling - Action - Outcome – Satisfied Feeling.**

Visualize something you desire and imagine that you are feeling satisfied after receiving your desired toy or bag or book or car or acknowledgement. Wait for an hour/day.

Test Yourself- Increasing feelings of satisfaction in all other areas of life would indicate that you have focused on the energy of satisfaction in one area of life. Energies travel from one sphere to another

Satisfaction in one area of life increases satisfaction in other areas of life; whereas feeling deprived in one area of life reduces energy of positivity/happiness in all other areas of life.

In brief – Desires are often short-cuts which do not lead to the happiness you seek. To get happiness, you need to be clear on the deeper feeling you desire before taking action. If you plan to be happy and not just successful from the beginning of your effort-making, your success will come true only if it would lead to the happy and satisfied feeling that you have envisaged; otherwise, the desire will change overtime in alignment with the satisfaction/happiness imagined.

The problem of endless craving can only be resolved by aligning the energies of the 'feeling desired - Intention desired – action planned- outcome expected 'before the desire manifests, in imagination. The more you fuel feelings of contentment, the more your manifestations, work performance and choices would raise contentment in your life.

Feature 4 – *The Law of Creation of Happiness cannot be used to manifest* *happiness from desires which are not in alignment with your inner/core beliefs and values, as energies radiate subconsciously.*

Often, desires are carried over from parents, teachers, peers or friends. You may want to excel in sports because your father/mother/friend wants you to. However, if you do not like sports much, excelling in sports will not increase your inner satisfaction.

A test of whether a desire is your own or borrowed from another's mind is your own increasing happiness. If a desire is borrowed, manifestation of that desire successfully, would not increase your happiness much. You may feel good that you have made another person happy by your efforts, but your inner craving to be content with your effort and more satisfied with yourself would continue.

For example, if you like reading books but your friend likes playing games, you would find more happiness in reading books than in playing games. To increase your happiness while keeping your friendship intact, you would need to invest more effort into reading books and some but lesser effort to keep your friend happy. If the friendship breaks overtime because your interests are different, your inner feelings of increasing satisfaction by pursuing your interests with freedom, would compensate for the loss of energy of companionship.

But, if you ignore your need for happiness and put more effort in keeping others happy, your own positive vibrations would reduce and unhappiness will spread in all areas of your life. Negative energy will rule your subconscious mind & body, by your decision to sacrifice your own satisfaction for keeping your friend happy. Overtime, your friendship may anyway break, because of you consistently feeling negative, drained of positive energy, sick and upset ... If you want to retain the friendship, you would have to choose a middle path so that your happiness stays intact and you don't feel sacrificed. In effect, you would have to make a compromise where you sacrifice a little of your time to maintain relationships but do not sacrifice so much that you feel non-understood and exploited. It is necessary to focus on feeling happy than sad on whichever path you choose.

However , if your friendship breaks because the other person refuses to compromise, it is good for your long-term happiness as you would no longer feel drained of your positive energy by another's demands. Breaking a negative relationship is better than keeping it on for the sake of a popular image but feeling confident and happy after breaking up is necessary to maintain the energy of happiness in your future. If you allow the other person to blame you for breaking the relationship and drown in sadness/guilt, the negative energy will multiply sadness in your life; instead of relief, which should follow the end of a bad relationship. On the other hand, if you miss your friends after breaking up more than feel happier, you need to go back and compromise so that you restart the friendship to again raise your level of happiness to the level that it was before breaking up.

To be happier, you need to be careful that you feel satisfied with the outcome of any activity on which you invest energies in more than feeling sad about any sacrifice involved. A persistent focus on feeling greater satisfaction little by little, would increase happiness in all areas of your life, overtime, along with increasing feelings of being successful and confident.

Practical Exercise 8 (PE 6.5): Understand Energy underlying Desires

Focus on the most important ambition in your life and focus on whether this desire is yours or another person's who is dominating your life.

Now, imagine the situation when you have his desire coming true. Imagine that your ambition has manifested and you have all that you desire. Make the imagination real. Make it bright, clear, hear the glee in the voice of other people as you succeed, hear your own mental self talk of thankfulness, feel your skin expand to absorb the positive vibrations, feel your feet on the ground and imagine sending previous tension to Earth and feel the feelings of contentment spreading all over you .

Now, focus on the next day after the ambition comes true. If feelings of peacefulness and self-worth have risen, the desire is your own. Your positive vibrations, health, self -confidence and inner strength would keep rising overtime along with inner contentment.

However, if feelings of anxiety and restlessness rise, the desire was another's who was seeking happiness through your efforts. Your feelings of happiness would rise even if you satisfy another's ambitions, but the euphoria would be short-term and will fade away soon.

When the happiness by your work increases positive frequencies of others, your own soul does not get as much upliftment in frequency which it seeks through its efforts. If your inner soul frequency fails to rise after fulfillment of an ambition, i.e. if you do not attain contentment, your emotional strength does not increase as a reward of your efforts. As a result, though you get mechanical success, your emotional quotient remains the same and your intelligence or calibration powers do not evolve. Hence, the anxieties which you live with come back and you have to start working as hard to fulfil future ambitions. However, if your own desires are satisfied while helping others, your contentment, soul frequency and inner strength rise which helps you cope up more easily with future problems.

To have long-term happiness, you need to ensure that you spend some time and efforts on fulfilling your desire even if you have to invest energies on helping others fulfil their ambitions, as part of being in a relationship or job.

Feature 5 – The *Law of Creation works to create happiness only if you do not remain worried all the time and learn how to develop detachment to problems.*

The Law of Creation works to create happiness when you are more happy or detached than worried as an average vibrational frequency. Happiness is a positive energy and matches with your vibration when you have set your mind at a positive vibrational frequency of energy as your habitual thinking pattern.

9. Since, some problems cannot be resolved in an instant, being happy requires the ability to detach from problems to fuel energies of positive vibrations as needed for resolving problems. When you are detached, you are at zero state from which you can move to a positive state.

    To have a positively high vibrational frequency, it is essential that you let go of worries and learn how to develop detachment to problems. If you are sad/ angry everywhere, your energy frequency is perpetually negative. Happiness is an energy of a positive vibrational frequency. Energy has to move from a negative stet of mind to a zero/neutral state, which is a mental state of detachment, to feel positive.

    Feeling detached or peaceful while doing work which you do not like, would increase satisfaction in work which does make you happy; while feeling sad in one area would spread stress in other areas of life.

    Detachment is necessary as creation of happiness cannot be possible in every routine area of your life. However, as long as you do not create sadness in your thinking while doing routine work, you would continue to increase energies of overall happiness.

    These non-exciting or boring chores help in developing detachment or frequencies of neutral (zero) energies which are needed to cross over from a negative to a positive state of mind.

    While co-existing in a society with others, each person has to do some extra work which appears meaningless in the present moment but has significance from the long-term perspective. You cannot refuse to make this extra effort because you are part of a structure and refusing to co-operate would harm your health or efficiency. For example, you may need to do homework because your teachers want you to or you may need to obey your mother and clean your room. Several chores like bathing, cleaning, homework, accounting, cooking etc. have to be done to maintain balance in life and you may not get joy from doing these balancing jobs.

When you choose to feel more detached than compromised while doing the work which you do not like , your happiness would not reduce; but, if you grumble & complain while doing work for other people, your negative feelings will rise and reduce happiness in other areas of your life, as well

Hence, if you can do the work which others ask you to do, without feeling sad but with feeling detached/neutral, you would create feelings of peacefulness in yourself, which would overtime, increase your happiness & self -worth.

As is explained in detail in my book CREATION OF HAPPINESS, **energy moves from negative to zero to positive frequencies in every experience of life**. Creation of more happiness than sadness requires that your feelings of sadness are minimized and your vibrations move from zero to positive pre-dominantly, i.e. you choose to feel feelings ranging from neutral/detached states to positive/happy states of being. Feeling sad or negative activates the MINUS or negative frequencies which subtracts the energy of happiness out of your life.

Happiness increases faster, as an energy transfer, by a choice to not focus deliberately on being sad.

Practical Exercise 9 (PE 6.6) – Creating Happiness or

Think about tasks which you have to do and you find boring and cumbersome. Now, delete the image of boredom in your mind with an eraser. To erase the memory, view the memory first as a film of color with you in its center. Hear the sounds, feel yourself fully in the picture, touch the tasks you are doing, feel the boredom, hear the irritation in self, and note the negative energy residing in you. This picture would automatically be existing in your subconscious mind at an energy dimension. Feel the color of the picture. If it is black/brown or grey, see a vacuum cleaner coming from the sky and sucking the dull, dark energy out as smoke. Let the place in your memory be filled with peaceful colors. Replace the sad colors with light blue or yellow or any soothing energy. Now, to dissolve the picture in your mind, make the picture still, the memory black and white, reduce the sounds till you cannot hear them, make the picture blurred, remove the feeling of touch and feel yourself coming out of the picture back into your own body. You may see yourself as a child entering your bigger body through a mirror. The mirror acts as a filter by passing through which you would be cleansing your soul of negative energy. Now see yourself merging in your own body and becoming the BIG you, as you are now. Imagine yourself becoming taller as integration of positive frequencies raises confidence. Feel the positive colors spreading over the space of the picture and a soothing feeling coming in your body. Smile and feel yourself free of the irritation. Feel yourself confidently optimistic, in the present moment, as in the NOW.

This exercise breaks energy circuits of negative thinking patterns in the subconscious mind

Next, remake the picture with feelings of satisfaction or detachment or creativity or any positive feelings. In your imagination, enter the same event with double your size. Smile inside yourself for releasing hormones of joy (eg.

endomorphin). Now, do the tasks which you have to do without paying attention to the irritation. When the task is done, feel content with your work. Feel good at your effort and feel the joy. Increase your size in your imagination to feel the energy of happiness expanding in your auric field. Now, leave the picture with a positive vibration and come back into your body .Touch yourself in the centre of your forehead and again feel the happiness/contentment.

Stay with the feelings of happiness, contentment and success for five seconds.

Leave the imaginative scenario with thinking about these positive vibrations. Now, whenever you think about your routine work during the day, touch yourself in the centre of your forehead and the same feelings of contentment will rise as the touch anchors the emotional feeling associated with the vibration of contentment in the subconscious mind.

TEST YOURSELF- If you have visualized correctly, the routine work would feel less boring the next time you do it. You can continue this imagination till you manifest it into reality. The idea is not to completely get over boredom but to reduce feelings of compromise and increase feelings of peacefulness, on an average.

You may visualize another routine chore and imagine feeling the same feelings of contentment. As a short-cut of the exercise, if you are a visual person, you can visualize irritation as a color and replace colors of irritation in your mind with colors of brightness/ peacefulness. Then, deliberately focus on these positive colors than on the irritation. Whenever you think about the task and irritation occurs, visualize it as a color, ignore the feeling of irritation which you feel inside and immediately transcend the color of irritation from black /grey/ brown to blue /silver/ yellow or any soothing color of peace. Smile with satisfaction within yourself and applaud your own work.

Do not discard your feelings as imagination. Internally accept the feelings as true and acknowledge the moments of imagined success in routine work as your future energy plan.

Negative feelings cannot be completely eradicated, as night/darkness cannot be erased, but the energy of darkness in self can be minimized by deliberately uplifting soul energy through habituating the mind to feel neutrality in tasks which created negativity earlier.

The intention of this exercise is to increase positive feelings in the subconscious mind on an automatic basis. Positive thinking helps the subconscious mind to release positive hormones which overtime improve brain power and health.

Feature 6 — *The Law of Creation is governed by energy movement and is not governed by rationality ethics. The vibratory law will create negative and positive experiences automatically on the basis of the feelings which you accumulate, even if the negative manifestation is bad for you.*

Sadness in life is created by a continuous focus on problems of life. The more you focus on difficulties and feel upset or tense, the more you energize the accumulation of sadness in your life.

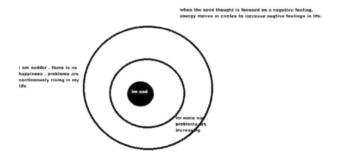

The Law of Creation ensures that every feeling which you focus upon manifests. For example, if you choose to focus on feeling deprived and suppressed, the problems which make you suppressed increase, overtime. Initially, you may feel compromised because your parents/relatives/teachers are unjust and mis-understand your behavior. This feeling of frustration would create resentment in your life which may affect your academic performance or general health. Overtime, this feeling of being suppressed would turn into a disease like bronchitis, asthma or you may get frequent headaches.

With a negative dominant internal focus, as time moves on, problems would rise .The Law of Creation would not create your reality on the basis of what is good for you. Reality would get automatically created on the basis of the feelings which you intensely/dominantly focus upon.

As you continue focusing on feelings of problems and resulting sadness, the same negative feelings would spread over the years into your changing circumstances and worsen your health and other deep relationships as adults.

Just as a virus spreads sickness all over the body, a negative feeling spreads unhappiness in all areas of life like a slow poison spreads and corrodes the being.

Your troubles continue to multiply an engine rotates energies from the point of your internal dominant focus. As long as your subconscious focus is negative, you would increase negative cycles of life.

Short-term happiness does come as a result of thought waves which you focus upon temporarily. For some time, you do get joy from a new atmosphere/ a lover/ close friend/ a new job but if the interaction increases with you focusing on feeling negative more than happy; the same negative thought virus which affects your mother and makes her complain against you, would infect your close friend/ husband or wife. You would create sadness just by choosing to dwell on it in your free moments.

To minimize the routine sadness, you would have to deliberately create positive cycles of life. Detachment from all that which makes you sad, would be necessary to let go of feeling negative.

To create positive vibrational cycles from your point of internal dominant focus, you may use positive visualization or imagination with feeling positive as a tool. For example, you can try imagining a happy situation which is opposite of your current problematic situation. For some moments every day, energize an imagined future reality by creating visions, sounds and feelings of happiness in areas which sadden you now. Focus on the imagined positive energy more than on a negative present reality by feeling happy while focusing on detachment. Keep thinking about how it would be to be free of problematic circumstances and the negative energies in your near and dear people.

Once you train your mind to switch focus to a positive feeling, the negative energy virus would die of negligence just as a plant dies in a desert. By choosing to feel good, you would learn to ignore a negative person by staying detached from his/her abuses by focusing on your own inner happiness.

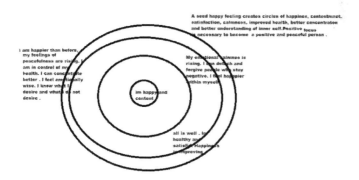

Overtime, the feelings of unhappiness inside you would dissolve and you would no longer attract people or circumstances in your life which make you feel guilty of being happy or dis-respected. Thus, when you start changing your inner focus to be happier by choice to stay away from being sad, your happiness would start rising in all areas of life.

Practical Exercise 10 (PE 6.7) – Develop Awareness of Transfer of Negative Energy from One to Another

Focus on the most dominant negative feeling in your life and list the number of people around you who share this feeling with you or who feel the same way about their lives though their situation may be different. For example, if you feel constantly deprived of love/money, focus on how the people around you also feel deprived albeit in different circumstances. Focus on the common emotion and how it transfers as energy from one being to another

If you feel more sad/ sick than positive, focus on the most dominant person in your life and how s/he encourages your feelings of helplessness silently or verbally. Focus on the feelings of self- doubt, frustration or dis-respect which this person has and which make you upset with being happy.

Try to understand whether this negative feeling is your own decision to feel bad about life or is it another person's mind influencing you who may think and behave very differently from who you like to be?

Is your focus on this negative feeling creating sadness in some other areas of your life? If this negative feeling did not exist, would you feel sad in those other areas of life?

Choose to disconnect from the people who create this negative feeling in you for a few minutes every day. Imagine yourself in a ball of sunlight for two minutes every day where you are loved by God and no negative thought/energy can come in. Ideal time to insulate yourself is before sleeping at night and as soon as you get up, i.e. in semi-drowsy states where your mind is too tired to think and prefers a break/ brake...In these two minutes, just breathe in and out and smile in imagined bliss. If you like to visualize, inhale white/golden white light and exhale out grey/black energy (also, try the Energy Cord Cutting Exercise given in my book EMOTIONAL MANAGEMENT) Apply a STOP on negative thinking for a few minutes deliberately by focusing on breathing or exercising.

Replace the unhappy person's dominance by choosing to talk positively to self or meditating and taking God's energies inside yourself. Also, mentally disconnect from the energies of sad or abusive people whenever negative feelings rise in you. Imagine yourself double the size of the negative person and fill white light in place of the image of the negative person in your mind. Overtime, as you keep focusing on disconnecting from the negative energy and replacing it with positive, the ability to detach from negative thinking would increase. With your choice to not feel negative, your focus on sadness would reduce and you will start feeling happier, along with choosing a change of circumstances involuntarily.

The Law of Creation has to be used with deliberate intention to feel more positive than negative, even if it means ignoring /mentally dis-connecting/ emotionally detaching from sad or angry people who maybe dominant in your life.

Since, the automatic transfer of energies does not follow rational thinking, you have to deliberately control your feelings and redirect them to focus on being happy with little things so that the energy of happiness accumulates and overcomes the harmful energy of negative thinking .Just as small precautions like wearing sweaters in winters keeps the cold away, small feelings of being happy constantly release positive electric impulses and feel-good hormones in the body which keep the negative thinking virus at bay.

Practical Exercise 11 (PE 6.8) - Generate Positive Energy

As a general practice, spend two minutes every day to count ten good qualities in yourself and your environment. In these two minutes, your focus needs to shifts away from self rejection or problems in your environment. These good qualities may be existing or those desired. It does not matter whether your focus is on imagination or reality as positive hormones are created in imagination as in reality. It is not your present scenario but the generation of positive hormones which affects your emotional reality/happiness in the future.

You may imagine that you like your body (even if you do not), your intelligence, your dancing skills, your cooking, your hair, your eyes, your smile , your reading habit , your writing skills , your patience , your optimism, your perseverance , your generosity etc. and thank your soul and God that you have so much to like in yourself . It does not matter whether these qualities exist in reality or not. By energizing the emotion that you have them already, you will allow release of positive hormones and thus, sow the energy seeds for the generation of these qualities in yourself in the future. Also, count ten good things in your house/ work environment to increase the positive energy in those areas of your life. In these ten good things, you can add gratitude for blessings like electricity in house, clean drinking water, parents who care to entertain you, your friends who like being with you etc. . . . Again you are creating a partial imagined reality which will get co-created in the next few years as you persistently fuel these energies.

Note - During and after this exercise, do not crush the release of positive hormones by negative thinking. Do not start complaining about the problems in your life and all that which you do not have, for atleast ten minutes. Allow your body to absorb these imagined positive feelings as if they are reality, before allowing your old habit to restart the negative mind engine again.

Feature 7 - *The Law of Creation operates at an energy level which is affected by the matrix of other people's feelings focused upon the same reality. Your feelings will be influenced by other people's energies and may manifest sooner or get destroyed by the impact of other people's energies dominating your feelings.*

We live in a matrix of thought waves, which move as sound waves or light waves. The thought waves which have more energy/ feeling intensity overrule the thought waves which have less felt intensity.

In a group activity, the positive feelings which we focus upon can be overruled by negative feelings focused upon by other people. Also, when competitions exist, the same feelings are focused upon by several people, and the highest energy intensity wins .For example, if you focus on the feeling that you are being acknowledged by getting an award in your class for performing well, you may be competing with other fellow students who are also focusing on co-creating the same reality. The expectation of the student who is most confident that he would get the award is likely to win over a less confident student; even if the less confident student works harder. A poorer quality performance may win if it has more positive expectations of winning attached than a better performance with fear of failure attached.

The higher quality of performance would get more acknowledgement only where no fear value is attached as self-doubt and fear lower the ability to receive acknowledgement and prevent creation of positive cycles.

Co-creation of Reality is a purely vibrational phenomenon and does not directly depend on the quality of work involved. Often, it has been observed that less deserving people get more acknowledgement in society ; but that is because they are more confident vibrationally that they deserve the award, while the more hard working remain in self -doubt.

Likewise, when you start working as an adult, you would again face this matrix of expectations in any job you undertake. You may find less efficient people succeeding over you because they are more confident that they would and do not hesitate using manipulation to create fear or self - doubt in you. Negative feelings created by energy transfer of thought waves would reduce your confidence and your positive feelings will feel obstructed by entrance of negative energies; just as a car gets obstructed on a road by obstacles coming up along the way.

Every negative feeling which you choose to focus upon would act as an obstacle towards creation of a positive reality in your life.

Hence, to create a future more positive than now, you would have to learn to **insulate** yourself from negative feelings. For example, a fear of losing can be overcome by developing detachment from an outcome while mobilizing effort towards manifesting it. Detachment is an energy of ZERO or neutral frequency and higher in positive vibration than the *fear* of losing which is an energy of a negative frequency.

To remain happy over being sad, you would have to realize that you are a player in a game and you may lose in some areas while winning in other areas. The areas which you excel at would be your strengths and the areas which you lose in would be your weaknesses. Positive energy in your body and mind would rise when you focus more energy on developing your strengths while putting less tension into improvising your weaknesses.

A soul is like the ray of sunlight; where the Sun is the Creator and the soul is the Co-creator. Each ray is a part of the whole but distinct in its individual abilities and the brightening of each brightens the light of the whole. Just as all flowers of the garden cannot be same, all souls cannot excel in the same areas of life or derive satisfaction from the same measures of success. Hence, it is necessary to be aware that each of us would be different and have unique skills of participating in the overall process of creation. Just as watering each cell is necessary for the whole body to function well, the increase of positive energy in each person increases the universal flow of happiness.

The brighter each ray shines, the brighter is the light of the Sun and the happier each soul feels, the more powerful is the feeling of happiness felt by the whole group and subsequently, the whole universe.

To increase feelings of being happy, you would need to focus more on the feelings which make you feel content and confident; while reducing focus on feelings which make you feel incomplete and dis-satisfied.

Energy transfers from one person to another automatically like rain falls. However, just as an umbrella protects, insulation from negative thinking protects the optimist. The people who choose to insulate themselves from sadness and focus on positive thinking are always happier and healthier than those who chose to stay sad.

Practical Exercise 12 (PE 6.9) – Insulate From the Need to Sacrifice for

Satisfying Negative People

Concept:
While understanding matrix of thought waves, the basic concept to understand is the energy of Sacrifice. The decision to sacrifice priorities of self for obeying others, who are pre-dominantly negative, is often a cause of stress and tension.

Though, Sacrifice helps in soul evolution as it helps in increasing happiness in self and others; it can lead to soul devolution if it is done out of fear. Sacrifice helps in increasing positive energy when it increases self -worth of the person and helps in evolution of new consciousness over tradition but it reduces positive energy if sadness felt is greater than happiness created.

For example, you may choose to sacrifice less important goals for more important targets of overall satisfaction as when mothers sacrifice a highly paying professional career for rearing up children. The satisfaction which is sacrificed by giving up on money is reimbursed by increase of peace in the house. However, sacrificing is harmful when tension created is more than positivity created by the act of sacrifice. For example, if you sacrifice your peace of mind to soothe a negative person, you often end up feeling more stressed without the other person feeling as ameliorated. There is a sucking out of positive energy without it being restored back by increasing feelings of overall happiness. Though, sacrificing happiness and feeling sad is one of the easiest ways to resolve a difficult situation , it fails to uplift intelligence of those people who keep demanding your energy without paying you back through acknowledgement, money or help .

Detachment or *INSULATION* from attention seekers is a better method of sacrificing happiness for a higher evolutionary target, than becoming sad as sadness or complaining reduce soul frequency. Detachments help you stay neutral to a traditional perspective of happiness, but do not make you feel sad about compromising on your inner values. Understanding where to be sad and where to detach/insulate from others is an essential skill to apply when deciding to use sacrifice for increasing overall happiness.

Activity:

You often have a choice between speaking the truth or lying to yourself to keep a situation calm and make everyone happy. However, if you feel sacrificed by hiding the truth, you need to speak up for calming your own energies even if it creates disturbance in other people's self-confidence or deteriorates peaceful circumstances.

It is useful to sacrifice if your self- control , health and inner power improve by the sacrifice but it is harmful to sacrifice to facilitate the victory of competitive pressure, fashion trends, demanding parents , pampered ego values and traditional requirements where your feelings of helplessness rise by the sacrifice.

It is also necessary to be aware that, if you hide the truth to protect a fearful, malicious or negative person; that person anyways gets into trouble in some other way because of his own negative vibrations. Your sacrifice of your own confidence and positive energies goes waste in creating a happy environment because the negative person spreads more unhappiness after being protected. However, your optimistic/positive energy reduces if you are sad, thus degrading the overall positive frequency.

Whenever you are asked to sacrifice to pacify a negative person or situation: Visualize two scenarios.

Scenario 1- Imagine how it would be if you sacrificed
Scenario 2- Imagine how it would be if you refused to sacrifice

For example, imagine that your mother is always in tension and asks you to do some housework as she likes which is more than your routine responsibility. To do the extra work, you have to sacrifice your time for studying or working on your own chores. You decide to win her approval and sacrifice your work time to help her relax by helping her in a way which she likes. In the short run, your sacrifice of studying/work time for relaxing her may calm her but she already, has a negative internal dominant focus as she is always tense. Hence, by habit, she would take on other extra work and her tension would remain the same. However, your sacrifice of study time would reduce your grades/ credits and self -worth. You may start disapproving yourself if you do not study as much as you need for your satisfaction, your work performance would be poorer and you may, thus attract disapproval. So, the stress which you try to avoid by sacrificing comes through another route, your mother's tension does not reduce but your sacrifice reduces your positive energy.

On the other hand, imagine the scenario that you refuse to sacrifice to help your mother as she likes but continue your studies / working as you like. Your mother keeps grumbling in tension but you insulate yourself and keep studying. You get good grades/ credits and your self- worth rises. Your mother's tension remains the same but is slightly ameliorated when you get good results. Your level of satisfaction with yourself rises and you can contribute towards increasing happiness in a way where you feel satisfied while helping others be happy. Your refusal to do routine work which you do not like helps you do better work where you are skilled. Therefore, your detachment from your mother's tension activates brighter energies in you, than being sad yourself.

On the other hand, if you find that you and your mother become happier by your sacrifice, then, the sacrifice is necessary for both of you to reformulate your priorities such that the positive frequencies realized are highest possible, given all circumstances.

The same logic is very important for losing weight. Losing weight necessitates that you sacrifice the need to eat traditional food to keep your mother, your friends or others happy and eat only that which feels healthy. It is established by research that heavy food is difficult to digest and the negative hormones produced, lead to unhappiness in the soul. But, most people eat fatty foods to keep up with the traditional requirements of tasty eating and sacrifice their own intuitive wisdom about how to be in good health. The need to listen to mass wisdom over body wisdom can harm health if the people advising are more unhappy/ fat/ sick than happy and healthy.

Feature 8- *The Law of Creation will create circumstances on the basis of your dominant, chosen vibrations automatically and cannot be directed by your verbal command. To create happiness, you have to make choices to feel happy and not just tell yourself that you want to be happy while feeling internally sad. Happiness is created only if small feelings of happiness are focused upon consistently. By default, sadness is created, if feelings of deprivation are focused upon, irrespective of success in the outside world*

Happiness is an accumulation of positive feelings repeatedly focused upon. The more we focus on feeling happy by focusing on every small feeling of satisfaction, the more overall happiness would rise.

For example, if you eat a good fruit, you can thank God and feel happy. Later, if you get ice-cream, you can thank God again and feel happier. Then, if you finish your work on time, you can thank God again and feel satisfied which is a positive feeling. Subsequently, if you reach home safely and get time to play or space to be alone, you can feel content again and thank God. Similarly, if you get to relax at home and have less homework, you can thank God again for more free space.

Thanking God is an energy vibration which sends a positive energy impulse to the universe. This positive electric impulse enters a positive frequency wave which then gets connected to your energy radiation and fills you with more positive feelings. As you keep thanking God for every small blessing which comes your way, you would realize that you would have greater reason to thank God with each passing day, as your focus on positive vibrations will increase !

However, if you find faults with every situation of your life, your sadness will increase as time goes by. If you keep looking for imperfections, you would keep energizing negative feelings and keep finding more and more problems. The habit of finding problems and cursing God or self for the difficulties you face would increase depression and dis-satisfaction in every aspect of your life.

Once you are sad, you would enter an energy cycle of sadness which will create more circles of sadness in your life. Then, even if you tell yourself that LIFE IS GOOD and YOU ARE HAPPY, the feelings of sadness would not reduce as your inner vibrations would remain focused on feeling discontent.

Talking positively or preaching goodness never works unless it impacts feelings. Till you can convince yourself that your life is good by feeling blessed more than feeling cursed, your life will not perceive happiness. Happiness is an energy of positive vibrational frequency and cannot come in your life if your focus remains on feeling negative.

Our schooling system presently trains children to focus on the negative aspects of life so that children are motivated to fill the vacuum in their life with learning. However, a focus on the gaps/negative, by default, creates more negative energy in life and thus, reverses the intention of the schooling system. Students become habitual to focusing on problems. Unrest and violence rise as children keep finding faults by habit.

If schools train children to focus on finding the good aspect of every situation of life, children would automatically become more positive and peaceful as the years go by. They would automatically fill the vacuum in their life by trying to find the blessing attached underneath every difficulty by learning how to cope up with negatives for remaining happy, peaceful and healthy.

Practical Exercise 13 (PE 6.10) – Developing Vibrational Awareness

Focus on ten things which you do not have and desire. Observe the energy of discontent or dissatisfaction over the day. Does it create more happiness or more sadness in you? Does sadness create positive motivation in you to work for these things to fill the gap of contentment or does it create more tension, helplessness and restlessness? When desires fulfill, do you find contentment or do you remain deprived and craving for more by habit?

Note - If your negative focus is greater than your focus on feelings of positive motivation, your problems will increase overtime. Since negativity is magnetic by frequency, sadness automatically pulls more energy. Indulging in Sadness is like falling down a slope while staying happy is like climbing uphill. Negative energy is low frequency of energy vibrations and gets more easily created than positive energy. Happiness is positively higher in frequency and has to be activated by deliberate intention to feel contentment.

Now, count ten things which you have and which make you content or happy. Observe the energy over the day. Does it create more motivation to have more or deprivation that you do not have more? Does the energy of contentment increase happiness or sadness in you?

You will realize that the energy of having would increase satisfaction more as you keep focusing on the contentment you have. Your motivation will rise as you have more as the higher you achieve, the higher you desire. But, by focusing more on satisfaction than on deprivation, your overall feelings of happiness would rise whereas the opposite focus of not being good enough / not having enough would create sadness in you and reduce your potential further. The energies of sadness would continue to create discontent in you even after your desires materialize.

Schools impact human minds more than any other structure of society as minds get conditioned in childhood. A thinking habit is trained by schools and transfers to adult hood. Thought waves travel from the educated to the illiterate and energies of happiness or sadness spread by transfer of thought waves. Schools need to teach students to focus on the energies of HAVING with CONTENTMENT so that the motivational tool for education is positive and not negative, as it now is.

A test of whether schooling is spreading positive energy or negative energy is the level of violence in society. If violence reduces, it is an indication that education has created energies of positive vibration.

But, if violence and terrorism rise, it is an indication that our education system is focused upon training the students to become more negative, frustrated and restless as the years go by.

As the education system, focuses on teaching the students how to be peaceful and positive, by integrating spirituality into materialism, the students would grow up to be adults who are positive thinkers by default.

Students who learn to feel positive vibrations through every difficulty of life would excel in creating happiness with success as they grow up and succeed in creating a peaceful reality for the world.

Chapter 7 - THE LAW OF REPETITION

"Feelings repeat themselves around a point of emotional focus. The happier you choose to be in daily routine, the more easily you will bounce back to happiness; the sadder you choose to feel, the more you will be pulled in magnetic swamps of pressurizing energies. Once you fall, in sadness, it becomes your point of emotional focus and you rotate in circles of sadness and happiness seems far away. So, it is better to train the mind to focus on happiness and stay afloat from the beginning"

In alignment with the LAW OF CREATION, there is a LAW OF REPETITION which operates in the universe to help you co-create reality of your life. By the Law Of repetition, feelings repeat themselves around a point of internal dominant focus by forming cycles of neurological energy circuits, called neuro pathways.

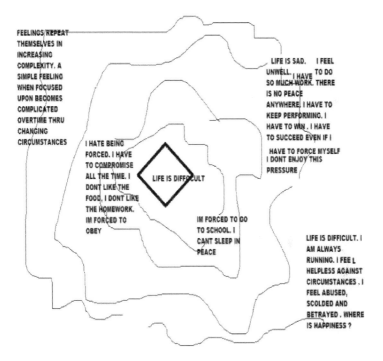

FEELINGS REPEAT THEMSELVES IN INCREASING COMPLEXITY. A SIMPLE FEELING WHEN FOCUSED UPON BECOMES COMPLICATED OVERTIME THRU CHANGING CIRCUMSTANCES

LIFE IS SAD. I FEEL UNWELL. I HAVE TO DO SO MUCH WORK. THERE IS NO PEACE ANYWHERE. I HAVE TO KEEP PERFORMING. I HAVE TO WIN. I HAVE TO SUCCEED EVEN IF I HAVE TO FORCE MYSELF I DONT ENJOY THIS PRESSURE

I HATE BEING FORCED. I HAVE TO COMPROMISE ALL THE TIME. I DONT LIKE THE FOOD, I DONT LIKE THE HOMEWORK. IM FORCED TO OBEY

LIFE IS DIFFICULT

IM FORCED TO GO TO SCHOOL. I CANT SLEEP IN PEACE

LIFE IS DIFFICULT. I AM ALWAYS RUNNING. I FEEL HELPLESS AGAINST CIRCUMSTANCES . I FEEL ABUSED, SCOLDED AND BETRAYED . WHERE IS HAPPINESS ?

The Law of Repetition creates sad energy cycles in your life if your core belief is that LIFE IS DIFFICULT. The same Law of Repetition repeats circles of improving positivity in your life if you believe that LIFE IS GOOD.

FEELINGS ARE SENSATIONS PRODUCED IN THE BODY. SENSATIONS RELEASE ENERGIES. ENERGIES MOVE IN CYCLES AROUND A POINT OF DOMINANT ENERGY FOCUS. FEELINGS REPEAT THEMSELVES

AS LONG AS INTERNAL FOCUS REMAINS SAME THE SAME FEELINGS REPEAT THEMSELVES THROUGH CHANGING EXTERNAL MANIFESTATIONS

The point of internal emotional focus changes four or five times in adult life, either through choice or shock. Your normal thinking gradually changes towards maturity and peacefulness over a normal course of evolution. Usually, your thinking changes because of external events which create a disturbance in your inner energy vibrations by planting seeds of new beliefs which make you focus about life from a different direction. These external events may include reading a new book, going for counselling therapy, encountering a failure, misfortune or a divorce, experiencing an accident, confronting a major illness, entering a new relationship, birth of a child or death of someone you loved.

However, if the person remains safe from emotional risks by making all rational choices, there is hardly any evolution of consciousness to a higher positive frequency.   In the routine course of life, a person's core dominant focus remains the same from childhood to teenage to adulthood. Therefore, the original point of internal dominant focus needs to be set at a positive vibration from childhood years for life to manifest happiness as the child grows up.

However, in the present world, the original point of IDF *(internal dominant focus of emotional vibrational frequency)* gets set at a negative vibration from childhood due to a focus on *what is missing*. Violence, excessive anger and rebellion in teenage, often, grows from forced suppression of negative energies in childhood wherein the child's mind is trained to compromise with sadness to meet existing norms of tradition or schooling. Suppressed negative thinking releases repetitive negative hormones in the body when seeds of negative feelings are allowed to grow inside the child and no attempt is made to maneuver the child's inner energy cycle to positive thinking. Simple negative feelings repeat themselves in the child's mind and manifest as complicated teenage / adult behaviors which are far more difficult to handle once developed than at the childhood stage.

A seed of being angry or sad which gets nourished in childhood develops into a virus of negative thinking which corrupts your whole life and infects the life of everyone around you. THE LAW OF REPETITION ensures that you remain focused on the same feelings repeatedly and hence, keep repeating the same reality. If unchecked, the Law of Repetition which is set at a negative IDF would produce repetitive emotional cycles of sadness in your life because of which it would appear that your problems are multiplying.

Once you start moving in a wrong direction of thinking, you keep on moving along the same road, by default. Your anger and violent habits automatically increase overtime and you become a destructive person who is abusive to others and feels sick within.

By developing awareness of the Law of Repetition, you can train your mind to feel positive by addressing and overcoming the need to stay sad from the beginning.

The seed of negative thinking starts with self-blame in childhood. For example, if you have the belief that you perform badly in academics, you will continue believing that you are poor in studies and hence, remain under confident in that aspect of life ; until you choose to change your inner focus with conscious effort.

A child who believes he is BAD and is constantly told that he is bad will become worse in the future by a repetition of the energy of this belief in his subconscious mind. The circumstances of the child would be manifested such that s/he continues to believe he is bad internally and suffer from low confidence. The environment of the child would reinforce the negative feeling as feelings repeat themselves.

BAD is an energy of negative frequency and will create more of the same energy in life. A BAD person feels justified in cheating, hitting and being manipulative since his belief is that he is *Bad* and he spreads more of the same energy. Children who are repeatedly told they are BAD feel angrier and become more violent in the long run as they keep spreading the energy of abuse which they receive .

The child who believes he is BAD may experience a change of beliefs and choose to prove to the world that he is good. Once the child chooses to shift his point of negative IDF to a positive IDF, he would start performing well overtime, or excel in sports or extra-curricular, to prove to the world that he is good but his success may include theft, manipulation and cheating. He would not radiate the power of positivity in his body and learn to be healthy or happy himself till s/he deeply makes efforts to believe that he is internally GOOD and spreads happiness by his vibrations.

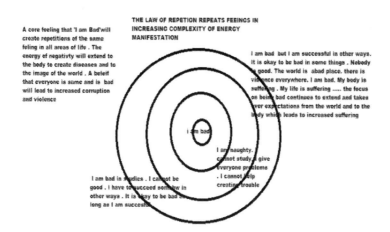

A core feeling that 'I am Bad' will create repetitions of the same feling in all areas of life . The energy of negativty will extend to the body to create diseases and to the image of the world . A belief that everyone is same and is bad will lead to increased corruption and violence

THE LAW OF REPETION REPEATS FEEINGS IN INCREASING COMPLEXITY OF ENERGY MANIFESTATION

I am bad but I am successful in other ways. It is okay to be bad in some things . Nobody is good. The world is abad place, there is violence everywhere. I am bad. My body is suffering . My life is suffering ..... the focus on being bad continues to extend and takes over expectations from the world and to the body which leads to increased suffering

I am bad

I am naughty. cannot study . I give everyone problems . I cannot help creating trouble

I am bad in studies . I cannot be good . I have to succeed somhow in other ways . It is okay to be bad so long as I am successful

Similarly a belief that I AM GOOD will create circumstances which will increase the energy of positivity/goodness in your life. Since the energy of happiness is an energy of positive frequency and the energy of goodness is of a positive frequency, the child who believes that s/he is good will be more peaceful, as he grows up. All the circumstances of the child would be manifested such that the energy of positive frequencies continue to make him/her believe that he is good.

BAD and GOOD are energies of opposite frequencies but every person would have some elements of both. You cannot be completely good or completely bad; but you can choose which energies you want to focus upon more. The more you focus on positive energies, the lesser would be your focus on difficulties; whereas the more you focus on BAD energy, the more you will attract problems and other BAD people in your life.

You cannot totally prevent negative thoughts transmission while being alive on Earth but you can control your feelings to focus more on happiness than sadness, by choice. Difficulties are a part of existence on Earth as the planet Earth is an amalgamation of positive and negative frequencies.

Your difficulties help you learn SOUL LESSONS which help you overpower negative energies and transcend BAD feelings about self into GOOD feelings by acceptance of imperfections with a conscious effort to focus upon positive improvements. The energy of acceptance is neutral in frequency whereas the energy of improvement is positive in frequency. You can move to a positive vibration only after attaining a neutral or zero vibrational frequency in your IDF. You cannot improve a situation unless you choose to accept it as it is, by your choice of focus and LET GO of feeling sad about it by becoming detached from the tension it creates in your mind.

Your immediate circumstances will not change by your choice of focus from being sad to being detached from sadness and happy about all that you have; but overtime you will be able to spread more happiness by your presence than tension and hence attract peacefulness than arguments. Also, a focus on good energies will make you move away from negative people and choose to stay with happier people.

However, if you choose to focus on the sad aspects of your life or the world, or past negative memories, the energy of sadness would create negative electric impulses and release negative hormones in your body, which will lead to development of headaches, anxiety and disease, overtime.

An internal focus on happiness will automatically increase pleasures in your life in the future while a focus on difficulties would increase uncertainties & problems in your future.

The child who feels bad or remains sad will keep repeating choices which make him feel negative. Hence, the child who feels bad about self may become restless, abusive, corrupt

and violent as he grows up to be an adult while the child who feels sad may become sarcastic, sorrowful, sick and under-confident in the future.

But, a child who is trained to feel positive/ content from the beginning would be able to overcome difficulties with a positive spirit and remain calmer in turbulent life situations which every adult goes through.

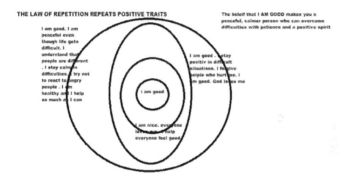

The Law of Repetition operates on inner feelings. The adult person keeps feeling the same way from childhood even though external circumstances change. The inner child remains as vulnerable and sensitive in an adult as it was in childhood and several problems of adult lives arise because the inner child has not been strengthened by giving love to one's own childhood self by using forgiveness, energy healing and therapy. Insecurities which develop in childhood dominate adult relationships until healed through the therapeutic technique called *Inner Child Healing,* wherein you counsel your own imagined childhood self as an adult.

For example, a child who is beaten by his parents would develop a need to maintain a false image so that he is saved from abuse. Such a child would continue to maintain a fake image as he grows up to feel successful in the world , because his inner childhood self will remain afraid of being beaten if it is found that he has been bad .

Similarly, a child who is constantly told that s/he is lazy by his parents or teachers would develop self -doubt in performing in all areas of life and become over sensitive in self-defense. For example, a child may be lazy in competitive sports but may not be lazy in doing homework or playing non-competitive games with friends. However, if s/he is constantly nagged that he is lazy, he would start feeling unjustly blamed and behave irresponsibly in all spheres of life. The Law of Repetition ensures that the child continues to behave inappropriately over -time because his mind gets conditioned into believing that he is lazy and bad.

To improve happiness and performance, it is necessary to criticize less and appreciate as much as possible.

For developing confidence in a child, the focus of parents and teachers on his negative traits has to be minimized so that the child can focus on his/her positive strengths. The target of growth needs to be *maintenance* in weak areas and *excellence* in areas of positive strengths. It is necessary to vibrate between ZERO and POSITIVE frequencies to minimize sadness and maximize happiness in life.

A child who is scolded unnecessarily in areas where the negative behavior can easily be ignored by a positive thinking parent/teacher; develops less in emotional intelligence. A focus on weakness reduces the child's positive power and s/he may, thus, not perform well in other areas where he can be excellent.

NOTE:

It is necessary to be practically aware that nobody can be perfect on Earth as the physical body is energy matter made by a combination of solid, liquid and air. Matter is made of solid, liquid and air and the transformation from solid to liquid to air happens by increasing density amongst molecules so that they bind together. Tension binds matter. Tension is created by negative thinking which releases negative energy. The physical body is the solid element of matter which is held together by magnetism created by negative energy particles. Therefore, to stay alive in a body, some amount of negative thinking has to be tolerated.

By tackling difficulties on Earth such that happiness rises more than sadness, the light of the soul becomes stronger in positive frequency as it helps the process of Creation as a co-creator.

If sadness rises more than happiness, the soul acts more like a destructor than a co-creator of positive energies. The destructor always feels unhappy and unhealthy as it spreads negativity by its internal vibration. To create happiness, the soul needs to create more positive energies in itself and around. Happiness requires effort as to be happy, the soul's intelligence has to be raised so that it can tackle problems of limited time & space on the physical realm which do not exist in nonphysical, celestial realms. The difficulties On Earth have to be tackled within the boundaries of the body and with limitations of time and space, unlike in the celestial dimension where the soul can travel anywhere at any time at the speed of thought.

In the celestial realms, the spirit is made of air-like substance and is at a positive or neutral frequency. It enters the physical realm to understand negativity and understand the difference between positive and negative emissions at a practical level. To enter a physical body, the spirit has to increase the density of its molecular atomic structure. Density is increased by adding negative energies. The positive, celestial spirit has to become negative to enter a physical body and it has to keep facing problems to remain negative as long as it wants to stay on in the body, as it is held on by the solid frame through using negative magnetism, which creates problems in life. The problems of life keep the desire to stay alive in a body, as the problems need solutions to move on which necessitate evolution of the spirit. If there were no problems, there would be no need for evolution either .As problems get resolved, the person becomes happier and evolves such that power and positive frequency of the spirit rise. Therefore, the feeling of being tied up in circumstances and the efforts to be free and positive again are a part of a soul plan to evolve.

Evolution happens by untangling the energies of problems which are created initially by traditional beliefs and negative thinking, that lead to tying up of free spirit's energies in circuits of negative thinking. By the use of fear as an energy tool, the positive energy of the spirit condenses and stays in boundaries (which the physical body represents metaphorically). The fear of death is induced at the conception point of the spirit so that the soul is not tempted to run back to the celestial realms when difficulties rise on Earth. Subsequently, negative frequencies are maintained by imperfections, tensions difficulties, diseases and other forms of negative thinking. Therefore, the negative circumstances cannot be completely erased as tension acts like glue which holds the spirit in the body.

You may desire your life to be perfect but that is not possible on Earth given your plan of evolution and the soul's purpose of needing to raise inner positive frequency. As long as you are alive, however hard you may try, there would remain some areas of life where difficulties will repeat themselves and some traits in you where you cannot be perfect. The more advanced souls have greater challenges as the greater the challenge, the stronger is the need for evolution.

Just as medicines have to be taken to achieve a desired result, problems have to be borne as side-effects of evolutionary challenges, to achieve a higher positive frequency. Yet, just as side-effects have to be minimized, the difficulties need to be minimized and happiness increased by a process of shifting the internal dominant focus to positive thinking.

As you learn how to change your inner focus from negative to positive in one area of life, you learn to practice the art of positive thinking. Overtime, the intensity of difficulties reduces in the area where you learn to be positive but the difficulties continue in other areas where your focus remains negative till you can shift your overall thinking to positive, by choice, such that your average frequency of happiness rises to being more happy than sad automatically.

A repeated focus on positive aspects of life helps in increasing happiness as conversion of feelings into physical forms happens through repeated energy movement in the same direction. Once you start thinking more positively on an average, you inner energy structure automatically changes to a higher positive frequency.

Once you start being more happy, by a deliberate choice to ignore sadness, your focus on sadness will start to evaporate sooner and your mind will seek peacefulness, by choice. You will subconsciously, avoid fights, jealousies and arguments because you do not like influx of negative energies. Overtime, by a repeated focus on being content or peaceful, the intensity of difficulties would reduce and be replaced by increasing happiness.

The Law of repetition ensures that your focus remains on the same energy cycle over a period of time and all your circumstances are manifested such that the focus remains the same.

However, it is difficult to change an initial internal dominant focus on sadness which keeps increasing sadness as energy multiplies in automated repetitive cycles.

For example, as a child, you may initially become sad that you do not have a bicycle, then you may become sad that you do not have a car and then you may become sad that you do not have a fancy car. As every negative feeling has an underlined positive intention, the focus on sadness helps you work towards attaining higher goals of materialism. However, attaining the goals does not automatically bring happiness in your life.

To be happy, you have to use imagination to create positivity and be content more than sad when the positive you seek manifests.

To use the LAW of Repetition for your benefit, you have to deliberately choose to focus on feelings of contentment more than on feelings of dissatisfaction for if you don't chose to be happy, you would automatically become sad as energy cannot stay in neutral gear for long...

Practical Exercise 14 (PE 7.1): Use the LAW OF REPETITION with Awareness

Everyone has dreams and goals which help you focus your energy in some directions over others. As souls, you always co-create. It is not possible for you to not manifest as that which you feel now, will come true in your future. If you have more fear, your fears will come true when your desires manifest. If you have more optimism, your happiness will come true.

Think of a desire which you want to manifest. Now, focus on the feeling that your desire has come true in your imagination. DO NOT FOCUS ON THE HOW. Only focus on the feeling that whatever you have desired has manifested such that your happiness rises and imagine that you have surrendered the HOW to the universe. The path will unfold as you keep focusing on the outcome such that you do not take a wrong path

Now, focus on whether you are feeling happy after the desire has come true. If you are realizing happiness, then continue effort on the desire manifesting by repeated focus.

To be safe that you take action such that your efforts manifest happiness and not sadness, you can also co- create the feeling of happiness in your imagination. While imagining that the desire is manifesting, also imagine that you will feel happy after the desire manifests. Keep repeating the feeling of being happy and surrender the desire to the universe (e.g., by imagining that it is a film which you have released into the sky).

Difficulties are part of being alive and would come automatically but your focus will determine the increase of energies in your life. A focus on feeling happy will dissolve difficulties sooner than a focus on feeling overwhelmed by problems. To maintain a high positive frequency of health and happiness, in your imagination and in your future reality, Repeat focusing on feeling happy and do not focus on the difficulties except while solving them.

For example, if you focusing on getting good grades in your exams, focus on feeling the excitement in your body when you see your results. Focus on your self thoughts, your inner smile, the smiles of those around you, the feeling of completion, contentment, the smell in the air, and the taste of sweetness, the self-respect and the vision of happiness. Make the feelings of happiness as real as you can in imagination, by activating all your sense organs. For some time, keep focusing on seeing your results, hearing self applause, smelling confidence in air, tasting food with feeling self approval and feeling of contentment with efforts. Then, release the desire. Do not focus on the feeling of worry that the desire

has not come true yet. Do not dilute creation of positive feelings with immediate activation of negative feelings. Deliberately start focusing on something else which is disconnected with your desire.

If you are not feeling happy after the desire manifests, in your imagination, then, change your action plan so that the happiness manifests. If you cannot visualize happiness in your imagination, it indicates that the desire will not make you happy when it comes true in reality as imaginations create life cycles at the dimension of energy manifestation. If your reaction is discontentment in your imagination, you can take it as a warning by your mind that your desire will not help you be happy. You can take the intuitive guidance and detach from the desire by choice to focus on being happy in the present irrespective of whether the desire comes true or not. However, if you have to continue pursuing a desire which does not release vibrations which make you happy, then you need to be more detached from the outcome, from the beginning, so that you do not feel sad when the desire does come true in real.

Keep a neutral focus when your inner focus is not positive. Whenever negative thinking comes, use it to solve the problem but do not dwell on it unnecessarily.

The negative energy is like fire. It helps to cook but burns if over used. The feeling of deprivation in the present helps to create the need positive manifestation in the future just as hunger makes you eat. However, if the feeling of deprivation is focused upon more than the feeling of happiness, on an average, the deprivation continues even after the desire manifests; i.e., you continue to feel hungry even after eating just because you have a habit of focusing on the negative energy of deprivation .

Habits continue if unchecked. Thinking habits require as much effort and awareness to change as physical exercise does. To feel content and happy, you have to remind yourself to focus on the desired future happiness while solving a problem.

Happiness will come with the desire you aim to attain when you keep raising your inner frequency to feeling the energy of being happy in your imagination while taking action to attain the desire. When making efforts to manifest an ambition, also focus on the solution manifesting and keep checking your vibrations for ensuring a rising positive frequency.

The LAW OF REPETITION will ensure that the feeling of happiness which you keep focusing upon, manifests whether the desire can come true literally, or not. For example, if you keep imagining that you can fly like superman, you would develop the inner strength to help others in need and do acts of courage more than other people who do not desire to be superman.

In Summary:

Every thought or action which you indulge in needs to release more positive feeling in you than negative feeling, for your happiness and good health to rise in the future. Due to the Law of Repetition, every feeling which you focus upon inadvertently, converts into form so that it can be experienced on the physical plane as a reality.

A happy reality is co-created by focusing deliberately on happy feelings more than on sad, angry, revengeful or hurt feelings. Happiness and good health are not an automatic outcome as is commonly presumed but an evolutionary test of the soul's ability to co-create.

Chapter 8– THE LAW OF ATTRACTION

Happiness gets attracted to your life when you remain in abundance consciousness and choose to move away from poverty consciousness with a deliberate choice to focus on being peaceful, detached and optimistic, while overcoming problems

The Law of Attraction simply states – *"Like Attracts Like"*

Frequencies of energies which are like each other get attracted towards each other and merge as one experience while frequencies of energies which are different in vibrations, separate. Energies are absorbed by each other or are rejected by each other through experiences of a life-time. All situations in your life are drawn to you or move away from you by the energies you create with your dominant vibrations.

For example, similar type of people get attracted towards each other as friends; while dis-similar people stay away from each other. Due to the Law of Attraction, people who agree in some aspects and disagree on most, stay together for some time, and then separate when disagreements rise. Alliances come together when energy vibrations are similar and move apart when energies mis-match.

By mixing, filtering and separating, people filter out energies which disagree and increase energies of matching vibrations.

Just as you attract people who think as you do, you also attract opportunities for studying and working depending on what type of energies you like to experience.

For example, if you like violence and adventure, you would choose a profession like the police or the army ; whereas if you like to deal in money , you would choose to do business and if you like to help people learn, you would choose work like that of a teacher, a doctor or counselor . You would attract energies of circumstances which make you choose a work experience which you desire to vibrate with in your life.

In abstract terms, '*Like or similar*" frequencies of energies match each other. Metaphorically, the energies of water and stones do not mix with each other. Similarly, people who think very differently do not like to mingle with each other. If water is poured on a stone, it washes away. Likewise, if wisdom is poured on a conventionally rigid mind, it gets rejected.

However, when water mixes with water, quantum of water increases; just as wisdom poured on an evolving mind increases the wisdom of the person receiving and overall wisdom increases .Contrarily, water gets absorbed in mud and becomes muddy water, just as wisdom poured on negative people can make the wise person self -doubt and become negative himself.

The Law of Attraction mixes energies of similar

frequencies. This mixing of energies aids in creation of complexities. Matching feelings create more of the same energy or reformulate the existing energy.

In the above example, clear water becomes more if increased with same type of clear water, dirty water when mixed with mud and remains untouched if mixed with stone. If we replace water with wisdom, we can prove that wisdom increases if poured on evolving minds, wisdom becomes negative if wise people mix with negative people and wisdom remains unabsorbed if poured on traditionally rigid people. In other words, the energy of water/ wisdom is reformulated when mixed with another energy which absorbs its energies as its own but remains unchanged when mixed with an energy which is too different, as stone or a rigid mind is.

All energies do not match. Similarly, definitions of happiness mis-match. Different people focus on different desires and dreams which become their future expected frequency. In accordance with desired future dreams, people vibrate on different frequencies of present feelings; thus accepting or rejecting the energies of feelings which others focus upon. Since energy requirements vary amongst different people, ambitions are differently defined in each person's subconscious mind; as all ambitions are manifestations/formations of desired feelings/energy experiences.

Redefining Success becomes necessary as achieving the same desires does not give as much happiness or satisfaction for everyone.

Therefore, when education/society insists on same definitions of success for all, several people become unhappy because they are forced to be successful in uniform ways which are set by conventional wisdom and restrict the range of frequencies of happiness which can be otherwise, experienced. Several individuals feel bound in chains of conventional life and seek freedom to experience higher levels of exhilaration which would lead to experiences of energy frequencies that offer greater highs and falls. When restricted by fear of falling/ failing by the more traditional older people, these children or adults stay in modes of unhappiness or rebellion.

For example, some children remain unhappy because they are forced to study whereas other children like studying; similarly, several adults remain unhappy because they are forced to stay in a marriage whereas others like committed relationships.

Blind obedience to old norms of wisdom and compromise with suffering in the short run for benefit in the long run is recommended for long term happiness, by traditional doctrines of thinking. However, just using discipline and teaching obedience does not help in increasing happiness. Happiness reduces if feeling of sacrifice increases more than the learning created. If resentment becomes more than pleasure, internal fights create more disharmony than positivity in the long run.

When a route of thinking towards happiness fails to take a person to its destination, the route has to be changed.

As experience has shown, the traditional struggling mode has failed to increase happiness, compassion and harmony in society. Peacefulness has eroded in the constant attempt to struggle for more. Violence, unrest and feelings of helplessness have risen by insistence on chains of uniform sanity. Focus of development has been on technological improvements which have left attainment of happiness to a trial and error process. However, happiness is not dependent on trial & error but is a product of matching vibrational frequencies. Happiness is created when happiness is focused upon as a routine vibration by a conscious choice to feel optimistic during pitfalls.

Therefore, traditional doctrines of thinking have to be changed to incorporate Laws of Vibration in their execution so that the happiness promised is achieved by the focus created & actions taken.

Whenever positive energy or happiness decline while executing a principle, thinking or action strategy have to be reformulated instead of increasing the effort, discipline and chains which people feel constrained in. Every activity has elements of negative and positive vibrations on Earth. To attract increase of positive energy which happiness represents, the satisfaction/positivity experienced from doing a job has to be greater than the compromise involved.

An increase in violence and unrest in circumstances indicate increase in inner vibrations of sadness and attempts have to be made so that the focus on being sad declines and focus on being happy rises again. This change in thinking necessitates change in choices of life. Often, it is better to stop temporarily and clear dis-harmony in energies than continue working with increasing negativity in thinking which can lead to increasing unrest, violence and bad effects on individual health. Breaks improve quality of work, as inner space rejuvenates sense organs.

If the energies do not clear after taking a break, the plan of execution of attaining the desired satisfaction has to be changed which may involve making changes in the syllabus design, or change of partners. To be happy, dissolution of a failing action –outcome strategy and evolution of a wiser action-outcome strategy is necessary.

The energy of happiness accurately follows the Laws of Vibration which have to be taught systematically instead of allowing a focus on suffering to continue, so that good health and happiness become a dominant part of routine repertoire.

For example, focus on feeling little amounts of thankfulness & happiness in every aspect of your life now would increase more happiness in the future than a focus on complaining & compromise, as energies multiply by focus.

The reason for bad health and difficult life are not external, but vibrational as manifestation of reality is an outcome of focus on inner feelings.

We, often, have to redefine success to ensure that happiness increases by the choices made which necessitates detachment from a strict, structural definition of success.

Defining success through good academic performance, a good job or marriage, without focusing on whether or not satisfaction is being attained in the process, is like building video films of happiness to please society but which fail to bring in inner happiness.

Attaining success for pacifying society's pressures but remaining unhappy inside, metaphorically, amounts to learning a subject without understanding how to apply it in everyday life. The Law of Attraction necessitates movements of positive energies to create happiness in life, but the beliefs & values which are needed to be happy are blocked by structural institutions which prevent free movement of definitions of happiness.

It is often observed that, when a person tries to be positive, s/he is suppressed by other people who believe in pessimistic, negative thinking. Dominant people's negative thinking transfers negative energy to the soul by transfer of doubt, fear and panic. You attract people and situations in tune with your inner beliefs and the more you suppress your happiness to please other definitions of happiness, the more you attract negative people's unhappiness in your life and spread pessimism by your vibration..

Just as obstacles come on the road while driving in speed, negative feelings enter a person's mind to slow down his positive energy vibration. However, just as a good driver overcomes obstacles with inner balance and caution, doubts and pessimism have to be overcome by a deliberate choice to remain optimistic while retaining caution.

If an advisory passes on fear, sadness, pessimism and doubts along with words of wisdom, you have to filter out the wisdom, absorb only that energy which you need and discard the rest . If you absorb all the energies, you would lose balance and become negative. For example, if you focus on self- doubts, you would attract the energy of failure. Therefore, you have to detach from negative people and just focus on any words of upliftment contained in an advisory tone.

Instead of defining success by the glitter of the packet/ your money income , if you redefine success by your happiness, you would soon be able to discard all traditional norms of success which serve you no more in being more positive or staying healthy and instead attract energies which make you feel uplifted, vibrationally .

Metaphorically, when water and mud are mixed and you need to get clear water again, you have to filter out the mud. Similarly, if you need clarity in thinking, you have to choose to focus on positive/clear aspects of life over muddy/negative aspects. To be happy, it is necessary to filter out sad thoughts of other people which have polluted your thinking with pessimism and instead expect the best life can offer given your desires & choices.

All entanglement with negative people cannot be avoided

as there is some negativity in every human being. It is easier to train the mind to stay positive and detached from negative thinking; than block negative people altogether as you would attract negativity wherever there is dis-clarity in your own thinking. . People of similar frequencies get attracted to each other due to the LAW OF ATTRACTION. You may attract a person who has similar frequencies as that of your own negative thinking but in greater intensity. Hence, some people in your life would be more negative than you are and transfer excess of garbage in your life.

In other words, you often attract people who think like you in one aspect of life but may disagree in several other aspects of life; which leads to friction and negative conflicts, overtime.

However, conflicts help in evolution of consciousness. You will be affected by negative thinking of others only if you absorb their worries. By fueling negative energies in your mind; i.e., by imagining the worst, you would attract the worst automatically.

 You attract experiences in your life by allowing yourself to worry as worrying is equivalent to creative visualization. You release electric impulses in your body while worrying which create negative hormones. Negative hormones depress your soul frequency and make your organs malfunction overtime, as in disease. You create the feelings which you focus upon.

The more you allow worrying about difficult aspects of life, the more you create energies of anxiety and attract experiences which make you panic more, due to the Law of Attraction . For example, if you worry persistently and feel sad about someone else, you attract sad experiences in your own life as you automatically attract the energies which you fuel in your mind.

It is necessary to be aware that while solving a problem or a difficult equation of positive vs. negative future expectations, worrying is a total waste of energy. Metaphorically, obstacles on the road have to be crossed over with balance and not worried about when the road is clear. Instead, the driving has to be so balanced such that when obstacles do arise, the driver retains his balance with clarity in thinking and does not get pulled into an accident by getting panicky.

To be happy in the future, it is essential to be non-negative in the present. You will attract happiness when your average **internal dominant focus** is subconsciously led to a positive frequency of energy vibration.

In applied terms, if you want to attract more, you have to create small energies of having the same, in your mind now, before you can experience having more. For example, if you want to attract more peace, you have to practice being in more peace in your imagination than focus on fights, before more peace actually comes in. Similarly, if you want more abundance, you have to redirect your feelings to be in the vibration of being in abundance, persistently, in your mind.

People automatically activate the *Law of Attraction* when they desire something with a strong belief that they will have the same outcome. Action to attain the desire is taken after the feeling is activated that the desire can come true. Strong beliefs create vibrations of strong intensity which propel energy movement towards manifestation of a desire.

People use wrongly the *Law of Attraction* by desiring something which they believe is impossible to achieve. For example, if you want to drive a flying car, you would know that it is impossible to achieve the desire in present context, and thus, not energize the creation.

Pessimism blocks manifestation. For example, if you are negative, you would be sure that a creation cannot manifest, and emit negative frequencies which prevent the attraction of positive frequencies necessary for the creation of the desire. So, you will delay the manufacturing of a flying car if you insist on believing that it cannot be.

The more you can believe in an experience, the closer you come to activating it through similar feeling experiences in your life. For example, if you imagine that you are flying in a car often, you may soon be travelling more often in aero planes or you may shift to a place where travelling is faster.

By the Law of Creation, it is not the literal imagination which manifests but the feeling underneath the visual imagination which gets manifested by persistent focus. The visual imagination of flying in a car creates feelings of travelling in speed, being free of traffic jams etc., and these feelings can come true in your near future if you believe in your imagination and emit strong vibrational thought-waves. You may even shift to a place where roads are less congested or get a new car which travels at a greater speed.

A test of whether your belief is positive or not are the feelings which get created in your near future. If you can focus on flying cars, you would soon be feeling more relaxed while travelling.

Whenever you can activate the imagination without denying its possibility, the imagination manifests over a period of lime; like the mobile phones and computers were imaginations, about a hundred years ago but have become a reality now.

The Law of Attraction, starts working by its effect on human feelings before a desired physical reality literally manifests.

By consistently being in a positive vibration, circumstances change so that the soul's positive vibrations continue to increase. Overtime, your spirit attracts the type of people who can get you the desires you seek to experience subconsciously. Likewise, your spirit sends away people who no longer vibe with your desires, due to a mis-match of vibrational frequencies.

Just as the Law of Attraction creates changes in your environment, The *Law of Attraction* is also responsible for changes in a person over a period of time. Each person changes depending on the type of energies/ feelings which he allows to stay inside his mind and affect his vibrational frequencies. People move away from you largely due to core differences in thinking.

For example, if good people mix with very bad people, their preference would be to stay apart. However, if good people mix with some naughty people, they would allow some naughtiness to come inside them. Once the energy of goodness is absorbed by energy of naughtiness, the whole group would become naughty. Overtime, the good energies may be able to convert the naughty energies into good by filtering out negative thinking. A negative person can become positive by allowing positive thinking to enter his thinking frequencies

However, a positive person can also become negative by allowing thinking of a negative person to over-rule his sensibilities.

(Because of the Law of Attraction, you lose friends as your vibrational frequency changes. Often, people who become negative with life want childhood friends back to feel positive again. But, if you want old friends back, they can return in your life only if you're thinking matches with their mind-set again. If you have become negative, positive people would irritate you and if you have become more positive, negative people would drain you. When thinking does not match anymore, you would get bored or sad by living with the people who you knew well earlier.

Just as you cannot go back to being a younger YOU physically, you cannot go back to a previous YOU emotionally as your soul's vibrational frequency shifts. Ideally, age should help you increase your soul's vibrational frequency to being more positive, wiser and confident, with your choices.)

The Law OF ATTRACTION ensures that only energies of similar frequencies mix with each other. It represents the conflict of the mind and the heart but it's always the core vibrations focused upon which dominate life, and not what the mind says.

Practical Exercise 15 (PE 8.1): Attract Friends You Desire

To create any desired outcome, you have to focus on the energy which you are focusing upon and change its intensity to match that of the energy which you want to attract in your life.

For example:
If you want some specific friends, you need to imagine thinking like that type of person as energies of like frequencies attract each other.

Activity - To attract a friend, think like him or her and support his or her thinking publicly in some way. Support would increase energies of attraction.

Practical Exercise 16 (PE 8.2): Integrate good qualities from people of opposite temperament

Everyone who does not think like you is not necessarily a bad person. Each person would have some good and bad qualities. People admire others who have qualities which they desire in self.

The Law of Attraction governs attainment of your desires in real life. If you need qualities in yourself which you do not have, you may get attracted to a person who is opposite you in temperament.

When you desire some person's help in your life who is opposite your temperament, you need to resonate with his/her thinking in some area so that his/her energy merges with your thinking on at least one vibrational point.

Once energies start matching, you would pick up each other's attributes, as needed.

It is said that "Opposites Attract" but such myths are meaningless unless the science/logic underneath the myth is understood. Opposite poles attract in a magnet and like poles repel in a magnet. But when we are dealing with people and energies, we need to remember that LIKE FREQUENCIES ATTRACT and Opposite frequencies stay apart as stone and water do.

Practical Exercise 17(PE 8.3): Break Relationships with People who you disagree with

To break relationships, openly disagree in thinking. Your friends would stay with you only as long as they feel supported by you. Once there is disagreement in thinking, friends move apart.

Likewise, you would move away from friends who do not think like you, as you evolve. Energies of unlike frequencies stay away from each other as there is no common merging vibrational point. Very often, people in deep relationships get divorced as their thinking becomes very different from each other, when each evolves differently while coping up in his own circumstances.

Practical Exercise 18(PE 8.4): Attract a Working Position Which You Desire

If you want to attract a position in your school or a job in adult life, you need to create the attributes needed by that position inside you such that you attract the energies of getting your desire. The attributes which you need may not be purely academic or professional. You may also need personality traits specific to that position which would make you suitable for that role which you desire to play in your life.

For example, suppose you want to become the monitor of your class or the supervisor in some work assigned to a team. The energy of a leader which you want in your life would be optimistic, confident, strong in positive vibrational energy transfer, accommodating to rules, sincere in responsibility and smart in execution. Leaders require more inner strength and optimism than followers as the leaders take decisions for several and are responsible for failure of all if the plan flops.

If you have adequate positive energies already, you can visualize the feelings of being a leader to send out energy vibrations of being a monitor in the future .Your present feelings create future experiences. The more you focus on the feelings that you desire to have in the future, the more your inner self changes subconsciously to become the person who you want to be. Manifestation of a focused desire will happen sooner or later.

If you do not have the positive thinking attributes of a monitor or leader, you would have to focus on creating these thinking habits in your life before desiring to be a plan maker/changer, as your desired position would call for these attributes.

The seed of a thought helps it grow by repeated focus. To create desired thinking habits in your life, you have to keep imagining that you are in that positive feeling experience much before the reality manifests. Imagination will activate the required brain areas to release the necessary electric impulses which would, overtime, create the desired attributes in your life. Your action strategy will subconsciously be motivated by your thinking ability.

The LAW OF ATTRACTION helps you attract the energies necessary for your desires to come true over a period of time. As you keep focusing on having the desired feelings of self - confidence, your energies may lead you to read new books, take therapeutic healing, exercise physically or attend seminars which help you generate self confidence

Practical exercise 19 (PE 8.5): Improve eating habits

Imagine eating healthy food which is not too difficult on your taste buds. If you imagine too difficult experiences, your energy will reject them as water rejects being absorbed by stone. Instead, imagine eating foods which you can like if cooked according to your taste.

Imagine the biting and swallowing and feeling happy afterwards. Create the energy of satisfaction inside you and smile. Do this for five seconds. After that, let go.

Now, you will either attract a food in your life which is healthy for you or you will feel more satisfied when you eat a routine healthy food.

Test yourself when you eat the food. If you have activated the taste buds and feelings of satisfaction, you will experience more of positive energy than you did before. You would feel more satisfied while eating healthy foods after using imagination than before activating the brain cells of satisfaction.

Smile for a minute in every hour. Do this for five hours. Forget all worries in this one minute like keeping a ball of negative energy out of your mind. You can count 1-60 while smiling and feel relaxed. Observe your mood swings reduce after this mental exercise. After a few days of this experience, you would automatically be feeling more joyous in every experience.

Now, when you do any enjoyable activity, activate the feel of the same joy in your heart by forgetting all worries during that activity, as keeping the ball of negative energy outside your mind symbolized.

Happiness means feeling satisfied through all experiences. Happiness does not come just by taking some external action to be happy and remaining sad inside, as action without feeling positive is like buying a chips packet without having food to eat.

Glitter, glamour, color, songs and noise would attract your sense organs but positive internal feelings have to be focused upon more than problems during action taking for the fun to pass positive sensations to the soul, after it is over.

Without feeling happy inside, it may be useless to buy toys, go to malls, eat junk foods , play games , watch films or be addicted to cricket or soap operas on television. All activities have some element of pain and some elements of joy. But your happiness is an outcome of you focusing more on the joy than the pain involved in the task. Therefore, the contentment has to be deliberately focused upon and increased; while the energy of deprivation has to be deliberately diluted and weakened by reducing focus on it.

The negative aspects of pain are helpful in soul evolution as they help in balancing desires. The aim of creating a desire is to ignite your soul energy to co-create a positive life experience. Just as fire ignites cooking but excessive indulgence in fire, burns your happiness, desires need to be indulged upon only till inner satisfaction is attainable and not addictively.

Every activity has a maximum pleasure limit after which it becomes addictive or sickening. For example, you can eat only up to a limit, after which you start gaining weight. Similarly, you can shop only up to a limit, after which you start collecting clutter which harms your peace of mind. As the law of marginal utility explains in economics, the benefit from an activity starts reducing after a peak pleasure limit is attained.

It is necessary to be aware of your peak pleasure limits and stop the activity at the peak pleasure zone than continue in greed, as excessive indulgence would create more negative energy than positive in your life. Usually, if your hangover, headache, tension or anxiety rise more after the activity is over, then it is better not to do that activity any more.

You can increase your peak pleasure limits by choosing to be more happy than sad in every activity. Overtime, your ability to be happy would rise to a higher level of sustenance. For example, happiness increases whenever you smile in contentment while shopping over feeling deprived of money, feel satisfied while eating pizza and let go when you are full than over-eat, experience joy by watching films/cartoons/cricket and switch off television if you start becoming anxious; peacefulness increases when you like being alone in meditation to free yourself from external pressures but can participate, without complaining, in necessary activities when needed.

Practical Exercise 21(PE 8.7): Improve Focus, Create Gap-state

Try to be in complete silence after every hour off work or play for a few seconds, roll your eyes around five times to relax, look up with eyes rolled upwards and smile for a second of satisfaction. The silence will help you be free of routine negative thoughts and worries.

This gap-state of mind will help you study or work with more focus. You will be able to create a gap state in your mind instantly, overtime, and be able to shift focus on your work even when there is noise around. The disciplined practice will help you switch attention to where your priority is instead of the mind constantly running away towards getting distracted.

For Happiness and inner satisfaction to be created, it is necessary to use brain power to internally be positive and smile in peace, with awareness of the Laws of Vibration.

Smiling, medically, releases positive hormones in the body which improve health and mind power. The upward looking eyes prevent thoughts from coming in as thought travel in the brain only when eyes are looking downwards. As long as you keep looking upwards, you will be able to maintain a silent state of mind. It is not possible to be silent for long as feelings release electric impulses like breathing does. However, it is possible to maintain silence for seconds by rolling eyes or looking upwards at breaks. Whenever, this state of silence breaks, the mind needs to be directed to think a positive thought or feel a positive emotion like imagining a flower and smiling so that positive hormones are released. The more you focus energy on being peaceful or happy in imagination, the more you will create, repeat and attract positive experiences in your life.

For the time you allot to being in silence, ask your negative thoughts to go away and come back for resolutions when your allotted time is up. Freeing the mind from worries for even a second or a minute in every hour would be very useful in improving focus/concentration in the long run.

Practical exercise 22 (PE 8.8): Overcome Difficulties by

Activating Peace inside the Mind

Everyone takes actions to overcome difficulties but problems keep coming in circles of depression. Life appears to be an exam where you are giving one test after another while having no space to be in peace and relax.

When your life is difficult, you can focus on the energy of peace and happiness by using imagination. Simultaneously, start counting ten good aspects in your life every day.

If you do not direct the brain to be peaceful or happy in your imagination, your brain will automatically drift towards feeling negative. Explaining through an analogy, energy is like a car on a slope and cannot stay in neutral gear for long. If left free, you would fall down the slope as falling down is more natural than climbing uphill. Therefore, if you do not deliberately choose to focus on positive aspects of your life, you would automatically be tense about all that is wrong and has been wrong in your life and in the world.

Practical Exercise 23 (PE 8.9): Be aware of your Feelings and

their effect on Your Life

A test of whether you are feeling positive or negative is whether problems are increasing or peace is increasing in your life. If anger and difficulties are rising and you are preoccupied with tension, you need to check your thought-waves as you may be attracting energies which increase problems in your life.

Being aware of every feeling is not possible as feeling is a routine activity as breathing is. Feeling is as constant for the brain to be alive as breathing is for the body to be alive. If you stop feeling, you will die. However, if you are aware of your dominant vibration, you would know whether you are feeling more positive or negative, on an average.

If you feel positive about your life, you will improve peacefulness and good health in your life. Feeling good will increase happiness & confidence in your life, overtime.

However, it is easier to think negative than positive. Negative thinking is like falling down a slope. Negative energy is magnetic by frequency as it is dense and it gravitates the soul towards Earth. When you are free, your brain automatically starts thinking negatively, unless redirected by deliberate intention to focus on positive aspects of every situation. If left unchecked, negative thinking starts controlling the mind overtime.

Often, health suffers as negative thinking releases negative hormones in the body. Also, negative thinking is addictive and acts like an addiction for adults like drug addiction, smoking, eating fatty foods etc... People drift towards feeling negative just as they drift towards smoking or eating unnecessarily.

Positive thinking is like an uphill climb for the mind.
The brain has to control and kept in neutral zone before it can be directed towards positive thinking .Unlike negative thinking, which is like jungle weeds growing randomly; positive thinking has to be cultivated with choice. To be happy in life and not drift like a machine from one difficulty to another, positive thinking has to be developed and maintained like plants are grown with care.

Practical Exercise 24 (PE 8.10): Understand Your Strengths

Choose some experience which makes you feel powerful and start imagining that you have more of the same. For example, imagine that you have got good marks in your exams and you feel strong. If you have had good marks earlier, you can just replay the memory. If you have never got good marks, you can create a new film as a drama in your mind. Otherwise, you may imagine any experience which makes you feel powerful and positive.

(Do not imagine feeling powerful and unhappy as the wrong visualization will make you feel negative and anxious more than before)

Focus on the feelings of success, joy and increase in self -worth for a few seconds with intensity. Focus on the picture of satisfaction and smiling in self, sounds of others appreciating you and hear your own silent self-talk where you hear yourself feeling good, inside your mind. If you activate these energies correctly, your general feelings of self -worth and overall feelings of being powerful will increase.

By focusing on feeling successful, powerful and happy, for a few moments daily, you will start focusing on positive aspects of your life more than negative.

If you have been non-interested in this activity which makes you feel powerful, you may not change overnight. But, as you keep focusing on these feelings, your brain areas will start re-adjusting focus to motivate the self for feeling strong as needed. Action follows intention.

Over a period of six months, you may start enjoying the activities which make you feel stronger or you may learn some new concentration exercises which enhance your brain power.

If you like academics, you may find new study methods and start getting good marks as you keep focusing on the feeling that you are successful and confident, by deliberate choice in your mind. Otherwise, it is possible that you will realize that your strengths are in activities other than studying for marks and you may start focusing on developing those strengths than academic strengths.

Deliberate mind control towards positive thinking helps in finding your areas of excellence and accepting your weaknesses without negative self judgment.

Practical Exercise 25 (PE 8.11): Detach from Doubt, Increase Positive Vibrational Energy Rotation

When you seek to be happy, you create a picture of happiness, you repeat focus on this vision of happiness and you keep attracting or getting attracted towards opportunities which help you manifest this desired feeling of happiness.

However, you block your desires from manifestation by absorbing negative energies from your environment. You allow yourself to be sad when anyone scolds you and you allow yourself to worry about everything bad happening in the world; thus encouraging the energy of negativity to take over your positive vibrational frequency. Overtime, the negativity travels to different parts of your being and you remain sadder by choice to dwell on the negative.

All this while, you may be taking action to make your desires come true. If your desires are not as complicated as travelling in flying cars, you would manifest them by preserving towards attaining those goal. However, you will not manifest the happiness you seek by hard work only.

To manifest happiness in your life, you would have to increase focusing on positive aspects of your life in the present, so that your positive vibrational frequency rises in the future. Energy multiples through focus.

So, when you have dreams of happiness in the future, your mind work needs to involve detaching from negative thoughts and people. For example, if someone scolds you, you can dwell on the problem and choose to resolve it or detach from it. Take action to solve the problem when the opportunity arises; and meanwhile stop thinking about it. Be in the vibration of peacefulness which will be when your desire has already manifested and not in the negative vibration of worrying and struggling . The correct vibrational frequency will attract desired opportunities for manifesting your ambitions but a struggling attitude will multiply feelings of compromise overtime. The moment you stop thinking about the negative, the negative energy will lose its hold on your vibrations and your energy would bounce back to a higher positive vibrational frequency, which will have to be sustained for the ambition to be realized such that it manifests happiness & peace along with success.

Scientists have reported that inventions happen when they detach from worrying and persevere with a peaceful mindset. Solutions to problems come when thought of being deprived is absent. That is because the solution to a problem cannot come when you are worried about a problem and are in a negative vibrational frequency .The solution to a problem is an energy of a positive vibrational frequency. Positive energy can come up when you stop worrying, just as light comes when darkness goes out.

Hence, happiness is attracted in your life when you are detached from energies of sad people, are neutral about your inability to help, and work on increasing your positive frequencies with detachment and optimism.

You cannot help the drowning unless you are a good swimmer yourself or you will drown along with the drowning. Similarly, you cannot help sad people unless you are vibrationally positive yourself or you will be infected with sadness by automatic energy transfers.

Energy spreads as light spreads and becoming sad with the sad will spread sadness for all, instead of increasing happiness. On the other hand, the process of deliberately putting light on darkness by displaying how to overcome the sadness through remaining powerfully positive yourself, will reduce darkness for all.

The vibrationally scientific way to be happy and healthy is to detach from problems and keep increasing release of positive hormones in the mind and body by maintaining an optimistic attitude through difficulties, being thankful after you cross the difficulties and sustaining peacefulness after your desires come true so that your energy moves from a neutral to positive state as you move from one set of desires to the next, with each grade of life.

Chapter 9 - Using the Three Laws of Vibration with Awareness

The soul in each body which gives it life force also co-creates the reality of life by emitting energies in positive or negative directions.

The problems which children face can be reduced significantly if they are taught the responsibility to think in a positive direction by making the training syllabus conducive to creation of more positive feelings than negative feelings.

While teaching any work, focus needs to be more on the feelings underlying an activity than on the outcome manifested. If stress increases more than optimism, the overall effect of the outcome would be negative in the long run for the child, even if the immediate result is good. The work of the teacher is to ensure that the students learn with a positive spirit even if the quantity taught is sacrificed for a higher quality of understanding reached.

The three Laws of Vibration operate by default but can be deliberately manipulated to produce desired feelings of happiness with training. While the exercises for smaller children, as of primary school need to be simple and short, children who are older, as of middle school or secondary school can do longer mind vibration exercises for improving concentration, confidence and self-awareness.

The following exercises can be taught to students above twelve years of age.

When you have a desire and you want to manifest it, you would:

Step 1: Choose a desire you would be happy in experiencing

Without awareness, you would choose a desire which may be borrowed from your teacher or parents or friends but which you may not give you the happiness you are seeking. However, you would strive towards attaining this desire even if it makes you anxious and unhappy in the process of attainment, because you do not realize that the resultant unrest and sadness would be your own responsibility. Later, you would feel disappointed when you do not feel peaceful after attaining the desire, and keep craving for more.

But, with awareness of the fact that your happiness in the future is your own co-creation, you would choose desires which make you happy in your visualizations/imaginations before the outcome actually manifests. You would like to be in the experience you desire from the beginning of the process to the end of the process so that your happiness multiplies as you move towards your goal.

Choose a desire which makes you feel happy/ excited/ peaceful/ optimistic/compassionate etc. from the beginning of the process to the end of the process. Visualize clarity while choosing the desire. Visualize contentment as the outcome of the desire. Also, moving backwards in your mind from the end to beginning again, visualize that you feel positive during the process of learning and there are minimum negative effects. Visualize understanding the process of attaining the desire and visualize completion with satisfaction.

The stress on satisfaction would ensure that your desire is that which leads to inner satisfaction and not that which is imposed upon you by peer pressure. Also, if you visualize satisfaction as the outcome of the desire, you may change your desire or the path chosen if the earlier mind-set did not lead to satisfaction.

For example, if you desire getting good marks in exams or a medal in sports, visualize contentment while being rewarded. Feel that you are more content than stressed when the results come out and you have peace in your heart that you are on the path of justice.

Step 2: Activate the Law of Creation

The Law of Creation is automatically activated whenever you think. You activate the Law of Creation whenever you desire an outcome or worry about an outcome not manifesting. If you are more optimistic, your desire would manifest with happiness but if you have more fear, your desire would not manifest or manifest with sadness, as you automatically, create the feelings which you focus upon.

With awareness of your responsibility in co-creation, you can choose to focus more on feeling positive and optimistic than anxious, so that you create happiness when your desire manifests. If you focus on the feelings desired before taking action, you may change the desires you seek to manifest if you realize that they would not get you the satisfaction you thought of.

To use the Law of Creation with awareness, you need to create the feelings of peace and contentment which you desire before the vibration actually manifests in reality. Before you take action, create the vision of the feelings you desire to experience. You can make it as simple or as complicated as you like, without feeling negative after the outcome is manifested.

Feel that the desire is happening in the Now and activate all your sense organs- See the picture as if it is happening now, hear the sounds, feel the emotions, and make the scenario as real as if it were happening now.

After focusing on these feelings, make the picture as large as possible. Stay in this positive vibrational frequency and let go of the vision. Detach. Release the vision as a kite going away in the sky. Allow the vision to disappear. Ensure that you do not become negative after the imagination is over. Stay in a neutral or detached or optimistic vibration. Do not worry about its manifestation or the problems which you will encounter on the path. Only focus on the energy destination or the feelings which you seek to experience.

Step 3: Activate Law of Repetition

Without awareness, the Law of Repetition is

automatically manifested when you worry about a desire not happening again and again. Whenever you worry repeatedly, you activate the Law of Repetition towards manifestation of a negative outcome of happiness.

Even if you do manifest a desire after worrying, the outcome carries energies of the accompanied worry; the euphoria soon evaporates and the worry overtakes again. You cannot manifest happiness and stay in a peaceful vibration till you use the Law of Repetition with awareness to create small feelings of happiness and peacefulness in your imagination in your daily routine.

To activate Law Of repetition to be happier in the future - Focus on a positive feeling every day for a few seconds, before sleeping at night, as soon as you get up and sometimes in the day. After focusing on the vision, only repeat the positive thoughts associated with the picture and neglect the negative thoughts which come up as doubts. Doubts are like bad virus, which spread and obstruct growth. Dwelling on the negative is addictive but unnecessary.

Overtime, as you keep ignoring the doubts, the negative energy will lose its grip. As the negative thinking reduces, difficulties will appear less strong and positive thinking will start ruling over negative thinking. Keep activating the Law of Repetition to merge into the positive energy which you like to focus upon.

Step 4: Activate The Law Of Attraction:

The Law of Attraction is activated by default without awareness as you radiate and receive energies automatically, as souls. Without awareness, you attract the energies which you focus upon predominantly.

To use the Law of attraction to create happiness, with awareness, choose to feel more content while taking action than worried/stressed. When you desire something, you take action to make the desire come true. However, without awareness, you may become more negative than positive while pursuing the desire,

However, with awareness of the process of creation, the external reality remains the same but your inner feelings change by deliberate attempt to be happier than sad. With awareness that you attract the energies which you focus upon, you would take all action which is possible for you to make this desire come true in your life; but without feeling more negative than positive.

You would choose to attract more positive energies in your life than negative energies by focusing more on actions which make you feel satisfied from within over feeling compromised; even if progress is slower. Happiness is a longer route than success but gives far more satisfaction.

Patience and disciplined positive thinking are the key to manifesting happiness in your life as contrasted with just hard work and sadness which are pursued for getting instant success.

You would need to combine positive thinking with taking action while doing hard work to manifest happiness in your life; and you would need to be patient with yourself and give yourself time to rest so that you do not become negative and lose your positive vibrational frequency in the process of ding hard work.

Pursuing only work without being positive would make you negative and lead to health problems overtime. Blond pursuit of material things, parties and money leads to increasing disillusionment with life; as you would keep realizing outer success without any inner happiness. But, if you combine hard work with feeling positive and allow yourself to be silent mentally at intervals for taking breaks to detach/let go; you would arrive at solutions to problems much faster and be happier in the long run.

The need for eating fatty foods, taking drugs and using violence are all results of overworking the mind to attain goals of success without taking time off to detach. The mind needs to be given interval space every hour for a minute. The breaks from thinking are achieved by being completely silent and feeling only neutral vibrations of positive bliss as in meditation exercises given in later chapters.

Practical Exercise 26 (PE 9.1):Improve Concentration

Using visualization and silent meditation is one of the easiest ways to increase concentration. The following meditation can be done anytime of the day and would take five minutes.

1. Imagine exhaling all your problems out of your head like black smoke coming out of a kettle of boiling water.
2. Imagine a ball of light above your head and feel rays of light entering your head. Feel your head filled with this light filling up the cells like bulbs glowing in your head.
3. Be in silence inhaling the light and spreading it all over your body.
4. Imagine concentrating on your books with complete silence around you. Even if there are noises around you, your total concentration remains on the books, and you absorb the subject you are studying with interest.

5.   Imagine yourself concentrating for an hour by imagining the clock dials after an hour. Feel good while studying.

6.   Feel yourself absorbing the lesson as energy going inside you. Imagine yourself writing the main points briefly and imagine yourself recalling the main points whenever needed. Then imagine closing the books and relaxing with closed eyes. Feel the silence for a minute and wake up.

7.   After this concentration exercise: ground yourself. Imagine yourself as a tree and your roots going deep into Earth.

8.   Also, practice being silent for one minute with a smile, every morning as soon as you get up and concentrating on your books easily during the day.

9.   Practice being silent in your mind for one minute before going to sleep and thank God imagining that you could concentrate well during the next day.

This exercise CREATES a thought wave in your mind which focuses on concentration. The *repeated* focus on this thought wave would strengthen the thought wave of concentration. Overtime, as this thought wave strengthens, it would *attract* more thoughts of matching frequencies and you would find yourself concentrating automatically more than you could ever before.

Practical exercise 27 (PE 9.2)

For a more detailed exercise, use the self- hypnosis script given below:

1.   Sit straight in a chair.

2.   Imagine black smoke exhaling out of the top of your head

3.   Imagine a Golden Sun above your head sending its rays into you and golden light filing in your head.

4. Imagine the concentration area of your brain symbolically enlarging and absorbing more information.
5. You may imagine the concentration area of your brain as a garden with weeds growing around it, initially.
6. Now, imagine that the weeds are cleared by huge vacuum cleaners coming from the sky and clay is filled on that place, after which grass is sown. Now imagine flowers and plants growing in that garden in your mind in place of the weeds.
7. Feel the space and cleanliness in your mind. Imagine flowers growing all over your mind as bulbs glowing brightly in the garden. Feel the light of the bulbs and allow the light travelling down to your body.

8. Feel a SUN like energy glowing in the center of your mind and spreading rays all around. Breathe into the SUN for five seconds. Feel the rays spreading all around your head.

9. Send the light down to your neck, chest and stomach. Feel a SUN glowing in your stomach and spreading rays all over your body.

10. Feel the light going down into your legs and feel it reaching your feet. Imagine black clouds of smoke leaving your feet and light filling up your whole body.

11. Breathe in the light for one minute and smile.
12. Now imagine yourself studying with complete concentration. Imagine how it would be to have complete concentration. Create the thought wave of feeling concentrated and enjoy the thought wave.
13. Give the lesson a shape, a sound, a vision. A touch, a taste, a smell and a feel. When you use all your sensory organs, learning is more easily absorbed.
14. Imagine yourself writing or practicing the exercises given for a few seconds. Feel that you can briefly

summarize the main points for recall. Then, imagine yourself remembering the main points once the lesson is over. Next, imagine yourself remembering the lesson after a week and recalling it easily. Feel good that you have made the process of learning easier and more enjoyable.

15. If you do not like studying, imagine yourself concentrating while watching a television film. Then, replace the film with your books and imagine concentrating on your books as you could on the film. Feel yourself enjoying your books as you enjoy the film and smile. If you can concentrate while watching a film, concentration isn't the problem. The problem is motivation which can be addressed by replacing the film with books, subconsciously.

16. Keep replacing the image of studying in your mind with an enjoyable film over a month. With consistent repetition, you will start liking your books as much as the film. This technique of replacing a bad image in the mind with a good image to convert a DISLIKE into A LIKE is called a TRANSPOSE technique (This technique is a part of neuro-linguistic programming of the subconscious mind). If this transposing technique does not work, the issue of motivation has to be addressed separately.

17. Imagine yourself absorbing all that you are learning with interest. Give the imagination a film - sound, a visual, a touch, a taste and a feeling.

18. Feel content while studying in your imagination. Focus for five seconds on the feeling of contentment. Make the picture big, bright and welcoming. Feel Yourself "I can do it"

19. Then feel yourself like a tree and your roots going deep into Earth.

20. Stay grounded for five seconds and open your eyes.

Do this every day for a month. Within a week, your concentration will start improving. With consistent practice, you will be concentrating automatically in about six months to a year.

Before trying any self disciplining exercise on concentration, analyze the motivation level and the desire to succeed to be happy...

All children do not study well. Everyone is not meant to be a teacher or doctor. Those who are not motivated to study, would pursue other professions where studying is not as much required.

Motivation is the key to success in any job. However, motivation is not the key to happiness as it can be controlled by factors outside the self.

Effort is worth invested if happiness comes along with success. If happiness does not materialize, success is futile and leads to bad health, depressions and temperamental outbursts overtime. Therefore, happiness needs to be the targeted motivational factor and not earning money or marks.

Usually, money becomes the criteria for success in adulthood by a focus on quantitative measures of success over the happiness factor. People become criminals, prostitutes and drug traffickers when they focus only on success without happiness; forgetting that just money does not lead to peacefulness.

If we stop defining success as getting marks in

childhood, success would not be defined by earning money in adulthood. If happiness is the measure for success, people would not sell drugs or guns for earning money.

People who are just driven to succeed become violent businessmen, actors and terrorists just because they get paid heavily to succeed even if their happiness gets completely sacrificed in their anxiety, competitive negativity and the belief that they have to sacrifice peace to succeed.

Other than self- improvement, the educational curriculum needs to be devised such that violence and unrest reduces in mass consciousness and there is an increase in peacefulness, good health and harmony by the choices made for self -growth by individuals.

163

Shiva Swati

Chapter 10 - - Daily Concentration and Happiness Training Techniques

*Training the mind to be calm to be healthy,
peaceful and happy is as necessary as
training the physical body to exercise to stay
fit, active and agile.*

Children need to be trained in staying happy as they are trained into praying in schools. Difficulties are a part of life. The focus of the kids need to be on positive aspects of life than on pain and suffering. The more children are trained to focus on being happy and smiling, the more their self- esteem and performance capabilities will increase.

The present education and religious system focuses more on teaching compromise over happiness. Pain and suffering are more focused upon than the blessings of life .However, compromise needs to be taught as a blessing than as a sacrifice as compromise teaches patience and compassion which helps in increasing overall happiness in the future. Just as you diet to be healthier, you need to compromise to be happier.

Prayers help each soul connect to God and sty strong in difficulties. Every school has prayer time. But, children often pray by learning words without understanding the intention underlying prayers.

Meditation exercises are more useful than prayers for connecting to God/ a Higher Intelligence/ Life Force, as meditation focuses more on feeling calm than just saying words of calmness. While words of prayer add more meaning to the feeling of inner silence, the practicing of silence, by itself, is a necessary tool for increasing receptivity in learning and peacefulness in mind.

Simple meditation exercises also improve concentration and make the children and adults feel happier as a routine choice.

Following meditation exercises can be used by adults and children. The simple techniques have been deliberately designed such that they can be easily incorporated in a school curriculum without dis-orienting the existing structure.

The following exercises would help significantly in improving concentration, optimism and a smiling attitude, if made a daily practice. The exercises are for kids from pre-primary to adulthood. The timings can be modified according to age group. Pre-primary children can start with ten seconds of concentration exercise. Primary school can do thirty seconds. Middle school can do one minute. Senior school and adults can maintain two minutes of silence and concentration.

Though these mental exercises can continue for longer, duration, it would not be needed in a busy school curriculum. For an adult, ten minutes of daily meditation in silence helps to stay rejuvenated about life. However, longer meditation exercises require huge mind control as the mind cannot stay in neutral gear for long. It either runs into positive day-dreaming or problem solving. If worries flood your mind when you are silent, you may need incorporation of healing practices. You would need to incorporate positive, creative visualization if you choose to meditate longer. Few self- healing exercises are given in later chapters which can be applied to individual students or adults, as needed.

The daily concentration exercises are to be followed like a computer programmer. The seconds timed, the timings suggested and the wordings given are devised for optimum concentration. Controlling the mind is like controlling a flood. The exercises can be extended but maintaining a few seconds of silence is enough to create states of neutral detachment and optimism in the subconscious energy circuits. In a thirty second mental concentration exercise, the mind attains silence after about ten seconds. We end the process at the point of continuing attainment of success in being silent and before the mind drifts off to being worried again, so that the mind is reinforced into continuing the practice of detachment, on an everyday basis. As students start liking the exercise, over a period of six months, they would learn to do it themselves for longer periods and incorporate positive visualizations.

Do not reject the process because it appears too new. Try these exercises for a week or a month to see the difference in attitudes of children. You will find more obedience, openness and smiles.

Do not discontinue the exercise abruptly as that will create opposite feelings. If you discontinue, tell the children that they can continue the exercise on their own if they choose to.

The instructor needs to speak in a melodious, calm voice which radiates peacefulness along with the tone of instructional authority.

Practical Exercise 28 (PE 10.1)- Thirty seconds LOOK UP

EXERCISE 1: Prayer Time

In prayer time, start with thirty seconds of breathing exercise.

Make the children watch their ears and feel the breathing go in and out continuously for thirty seconds with their eyes looking upwards, before starting the prayers. This will help the blood flow more to the brains and remove sleepiness.

Positive effect – Getting in touch with breathing is the first step towards accessing the inner self and understanding the subconscious mind.

Reduction of Negative Effect – Thirty seconds of silent focus on ears will help remove a perpetual tendency of the mind to chatter aimlessly and make the children like focusing.

Practical exercise 29 (PE 10.2)- Thirty Seconds Smiling

Exercise 2: Prayer time

Ask the children to SMILE/ LAUGH for thirty seconds while focusing on the top of their head (The crown chakra)Then, ask them to say **Thank You , Body, Thank You Earth, Than You God** and SMILE with love and gratitude for their own body and being . Then, ask them to **open their eyes.**

Positive Effect – Smiling releases positive hormones in the body which improve health in the long run. Expressing Gratitude helps the body feel better and more co-operative.

 Reduction of negative Habit – This exercise will reduce the tendency to chatter aimlessly.

Practical Exercise 30 (PE 10.3) - Thirty Seconds SILENCE

EXERCISE 3: Prayer Time

Ask the children to raise their hands up till the top pf their head or till their ears and simultaneously roll up their tongues to the tip of the palate.

Keep thirty seconds of silence. Exhale from nose and bring hands down after thirty seconds.

 Try to SMILE inside the stomach while keeping silence. Focus has to be only on silently smiling and no other thoughts. A clear, smiling focus helps release positive hormones in the body without distractions created by negative hormones released during routine, negative thinking.

If you are an adult and your mind wanders, keep a Two-point focus. Feel the smile and feel the breath inside the stomach. Otherwise, focus on your eyes and your feet simultaneously.

The energy of the smile travels to the stomach as you keep focus on the stomach while smiling. This will ensure you feeling happier for thirty seconds.

Positive Effect- A further release of Positive Hormones is activated in the body thus, taking the process of understanding the connection between good feeling and good health deeper.

Reduction Of Negative Side Effect - This break from routine thinking helps break energy circuits of worries inside the mind, which leads to deactivation of an older cycle of problems over a period of consistent recycling.

Practical Exercise 31 (PE 10.4) - Five Minutes Gratitude with Body awareness

This exercise may not be possible for children under seven years of age. Between the ages 7-12, you may ask the children to touch each part of the body while feeling light glowing in each part for 5 seconds, with saying ' Thank You , God'. After ages 12, ask the children to visualize mentally/ imagine each part of the body. Focused imagination helps to activate the brain's abstract thinking areas. For brain development, it is better to imagine different parts of the body than touching each part.

Exercise 4: Prayer Time

After the silence, you can add Progressive Relaxation for five minutes. For this exercise, use the following steps.

1. Imagine the top of your head and feel God's light on the top of your head. Say '*Thank You God/ Thank You, Life Force'*. Feel bulbs of light glowing in your brain. Breathe for five seconds.

2. Next move to your eyes. Feel God's light on your eyes. Say *"Thank you God/ Thank You Life Force"*. Feel a glowing light in your eyes for five seconds.

3. Next move to your Nose. Imagine God's light on your nose. Say '*Thank You God/ Thank You, Life Force'*. Feel the light for five seconds.

4. Next, Move to your chin. Say '**Thank You God/ Thank You, Life Force**' Feel the chin lighted up for five seconds.

5. Next, Move to your whole Face. Say **"Thank You God / Thank You, Life Force"**. Feel the ears, cheeks, back of the head and the whole face lighted up for five seconds.

6. Next, move to your throat. Say '*Thank You God / Thank You, Life Force'*. Feel the throat lighted up for five seconds. Feel the back of the throat also lighted up.

7. Next, move to your Arms. Feel your arms and fingers lighted up. Say '*Thank You God / Thank You, Life Force* '

8. Next, move to your chest. Feel the heart lighted up. Say *"Thank You God/ Thank You, Life Force"*. Feel the centre of the chest filled with light and imagine a heart shape there. Feel the Heart Expand like a flower opening its petals and receiving light. Feel the back of the heart expand also like a flower opening up to receive light.
   You give love out from the front of your heart and you

receive love from the back of your heart. You have to receive to give. Hence, imagine both the front heart chakra and back heart chakra opening up. Join your hands together, feel your chest expanding with light and love, **smile** and say ***Thank you, God/ Thank You, Life Force.***

9. Next, move to your stomach. Feel an imagined SUN glowing in the centre of your stomach. You can also imagine a ball of light/ a bulb/ a glowing energy in your stomach. Feel the light spreading its rays all over your body and all the parts of your body glowing with light. Connect a ray of light to the top of your head. Say ***Thank You God/ Thank you life Force and SMILE***. Feel the light spread for five seconds. Then SMILE and spread the energy of positive light / positive energy to your whole body ,

10. Next, feel the light move to your spine and back. Feel your spine and back lighted up. Say *'**Thank You God/ Life Force for your support** "*. Feel the light travelling up and down the spine for five seconds, and a lotus opening at the base of your spine. The lotus represents evolution and   the goddess of knowledge. Feel the energy of white light spreading all over your body for five seconds.

11. Next, feel the light travelling to your legs, knees and feet. Feel your feet glowing with light. Say *'**Thank you God/ Thank You, Life Force** 'for your support*. Imagine light moving up and down your legs for five seconds.

12. Next, feel the light going into Earth from your feet. This is the grounding exercise. Imagine yourself like a tree and feel your energy going deep into Earth like the roots of a tree. Feel firm in your balance. Say "***Thank***

you, Earth" and smile for five seconds. Then say "***Thank You God/ Thank You Life force***" and feel the energy at the top of your head again.

13. Next feel energy moving from the top of your head to the bottom of your feet and deep into Earth , again rising up to the top of your head and again moving down to get deeply rooted into earth .

14. End the progressive relaxation Exercise with a smile.

Positive Effect – This exercise helps improve the mind-body-soul balance, with awareness, that there is an energy flow balance between Earth and Cosmic energies. It helps to release positive hormones in the body, feel gratitude, feel supported and improve overall health in the long run.

Reduction of Negative effect - This exercise activates the clear circular flow of energies which is obstructed by negative thinking, otherwise. An interaction between energies of Earth and Spirit happens automatically but remains imbalanced without awareness.

Now, you may chant your regular prayers.

Practical Exercise 32 (PE 10.5) – 1 minute of cleansing and rejuvenating the soul with an energy shower

Exercise 5: Prayer Time

After the prayers are over, or after Progressive Relaxation exercise:

Imagine a shower of light/water coming from the sky and filling up the body with clear light/ energy. Feel stress flowing away like black water going into Earth. Feel your feet lighted up and your whole body clearer. Allow yourself to feel relaxed. Say "*I feel clear, calm and balanced* ". Next, imagine a ring of light or a shield of light around you which keeps you immune from negative energies. This energy shield will program your subconscious mind to reduce absorption of words, feelings or thoughts of people which make you feel negative/ sad/ angry. This Technique is called an ENERGY SHOWER.

An Energy shower helps is remaining healthy in the mind by removing stress daily, as much as a bathing shower keeps the body healthy by removing dirt daily.

Positive Effect- This exercise is very useful in removing daily stress. It can also be practiced any time of the day after an emotionally stressful situation or before sleeping at night.

Reduction of Negative Effect- Just as a body which is not cleaned, remains unhealthy; the energy filed of the mind remains unhealthy if not cleaned with concentrating on releasing negative energies like bathing with a shower.

Practical exercises 33 (PE 10.6) – Centering & Grounding

Exercise 6: Prayer Time

You may add the following physical exercise of deep breathing before starting the day.

1. Deeply Breathe into your stomach for five counts.
2. Breathe Out Slowly for Five Counts.
3. Deeply Breathe into Your Feet for five Counts.
4. Breathe Slowly out of your feet for five counts.
5. Deeply Breathe into your Eyes for five Counts.
6. Breathe Slowly out of your eyes for five counts.

7. Exhale from the crown chakra and breathe into your body. You may breathe in imagined sunlight/ healing energy into your own body and visualize it healthy.

8. Feel your feet firmly on ground for thirty seconds. Grounding is necessary to be focused during the day.

Positive Effect– This exercise will help in becoming balanced and focused.

Reduction Of Negative Effect – This exercise will remove swaying of the astral body away from the physical body as happens during day-dreaming, absent mindedness etc.

Calming Exercises during SCHOOL HOURS

Practical Exercise 34 (PE 10.7) - Practicing inner energy movement, 30 seconds

Exercise 7: School Hours

Upon starting the day,

In the classroom, ask the children to close eyes, touch their stomach, feel a light glowing in the stomach and maintain silence with a SMILE for twenty seconds. Then, ask them to laugh from their stomach for twenty seconds

Then, start the routine.

Positive Effect- This exercise will help the children start the day with their inner self participating in the process. Imagining the glow in the stomach will make the inner self come alive.

Reduction of Negative Side Effect – This exercise will reduce anger and restlessness. The body feels calmer when the inner self is alive.

Practical Exercise 35 (PE 10. 8) - Eating with Interest, Contentment & Gratitude

Exercise 8: School Hours

At interval time, before eating food, ask the children to maintain silence for ten seconds.

Say '***Thank you, Universe/ God/ Earth/ …. I like my food. I am happy***. **Smile**".

You can thank any cosmic force to make the exercise generalized. The younger children can start eating after saying these positive words as words automatically accompany feelings for young children. .

To create positive feelings in the older children, you may ask the older children to imagine eating food and liking it. Create the positive feeling of liking the food while eating it through using imagination in the mind before experiencing the actual eating in reality. You can ask them to imagine for ten seconds to make it a stress free exercise. Tell them *"Imagine liking the food in your mind* "ask them to imagine for five – ten seconds. . Then, allow them to eat. Encourage eating slowly as that is better for digestion, developing patience, weight loss/ weight balance and feeling contentment.

This exercise will ensure that the children enjoy their food more and experience contentment. Even if some children do not like the food initially, overtime, energies will shift so that the food changes to their liking.

You may train older kids to imagine a feeling of contentment along with liking the food, before eating. You may use the following words or add more words to the word 'contentment '.

Ask "*Imagine How it feels to be content after eating a meal. Feel the contentment now. "Say "I Thank Myself that I like the food I eat and feel content. " Ask the children to Smile.*"

Saying the word SMILE is a verbal command to self or the children, which would create a *smile* even if there is no occasion or no mood for smiling. The smile by itself would release positive hormones which would make the children and self, cheerful.

 It is possible that the every child does not like the food served as different children have different tastes. Ask the children to *"ignore the negative energy which comes up, if you do not like the food on plate .Overtime, your mind conditioning, food tastes or food servings will change so that you literally like the food you eat with contentment . Have patience"*

Positive Effect- This exercise will activate concentration and creative areas of the brain.

Reduction of Negative side effect- Children will feel less helpless overtime as they will realize they have a control on their reality. They will realize that the feelings they get into before the actual act, manifest in reality overtime. If they imagine liking the food before the act of eating, they will realize that they start liking the food more than if they do not imagine. The subconscious mind creates feelings in response to focus. When there is no focus, repetitive negative feelings circulate but when there is a new, activated, positive focus, the negative feelings are replaced by happy feelings deliberately created.

Practical Exercise 36 (PE 10.9) – Laughter for thirty seconds

Exercise 9: School Hours

After interval time, make the children to do laughter exercise again for thirty seconds. Ask them to laugh for thirty seconds while feeling the movement of optimism in their stomach. Then, maintain silence for ten seconds. Then, start studying again.

Positive Effect – Laughing for thirty seconds would cause a sustained release of positive hormones in the body.

Reduction Of Negative Effect – Laughing would reduce sleepiness and boredom by release of positive hormones in the brain.

Practical Exercise 40 (PE 10.10)- Count Blessings

Exercise 10: School Hours

At the end of the day, or at the beginning of the last period, make the children focus on two - five good things which happened to them or anyone else during the day. You can ask them to write it or say it. Then, make them say one bad thing which happened. Again ask them to recall the good things which happened and smile. Guide them every day to notice that the energy of good is bigger than the energy of bad.

Focus will change perceptions. Overtime, children would start noticing positive aspects of life which they ignored earlier as given.

Practical Exercise 41(PE 10.11) - Exhale Stress, 90 seconds

Exercise 11: School Hours

At the end of the day, or at the beginning of the last period, ask the children to do the laughter exercise for twenty seconds. Then ask them to say "**Thank You, God/ Life force** ", and smile. Next, you may ask them to breathe out the stress by exhaling from the top of the head. Say "Breathe out from the top of your Head. Now, imagine a bright, happy/pleasant light coming from the sky and filling in your whole body. Feel all the stress going into Earth as black water leaving your body and going into Earth. Mentally say *"Thank You Earth* "and imagine a happy planet. Visualize Earth glowing with green, blue and pleasant sunlight. Help them imagine trees growing in surplus, clean air free of pollution, clean roads, smiling and loving people and all that you want in a Happy Earth.

After having an imagined picture of a happy Earth, SMILE and maintain silence for thirty Seconds.

The smiling and silence will ensure that the children go home in a pleasant spirit. Imagining a happy earth will motivate the kids, subconsciously, to work towards creating a happy planet in the future. Current Feelings create future reality. Focusing on problems of Earth creates more of the same energy as energies multiply with focus. To create a happy planet, focus needs to be on imagining how it would be if the problems were resolved and a happy planet was created. There needs to be a greater energy focus on resolution than on discussing the problems for the energy of resolution to spread more than the energy of problems.

These exercises will reduce anger and increase peace in daily routine. The children would start smiling more automatically. They will also start creating positive expectations from their life more than feeling negative.

Chapter 11 - Structural Improvement Exercises for Developing Patience & Peacefulness

Patience is a necessary skill which every soul seeks to learn while on Earth. Patience helps in developing perseverance which helps in creation of a better life. Human beings have evolved over animals by displaying far more skills of patience than animals can ever display. Learning comes by applying patience.

Long term routine peace and happiness are an outcome of applying patience. Delaying short term gratification helps in obtaining long term benefit of a deeper quality.

For example, if you cook your meals instead of eating junk food, you get more satisfaction; if you exercise or move your physical joints with awareness and patience daily, you feel healthier than if you do not; if you save money with patience, you can spend more money over the long run and get more satisfaction than spending impulsively.

 In all these activities, the important ingredient to keep in mind is that the sacrifice involved in applying patience needs to be lesser than the benefits obtained. If pain is greater than gain, sadness will rule. Hence, activities need to be designed such that satisfaction gained is greater than pain.

The positive effects of patience need to be greater than the negative sacrifice involved, for happiness, good health and detachment to rule over sadness in routine life.

Developing patience is essential as it helps in creating much more long - term gain over short term gratification. All inventions which have improved human life were built on energies of persistence with patience. All good relationships require energies of forgiveness and patience.

Training children in Patience helps them cope with problems of adult life in a balanced, peaceful manner. Some amount of Patience is automatically taught in the education system. Children are asked to apply patience while studying, writing, eating etc.

However, children who are very restless find it extremely frustrating to apply patience and rebel whenever opportunity arises. The patience applied while studying often makes the children behave angrily outside school and several kids become rebellious during teenage.

There are a few, simple changes which can be made in the structure of education which would help children be more peaceful while studying. Other changes can be made in the daily routine of the kids to improve their desire to be patient.

The following exercises would help in increasing peacefulness in children and adults while inculcating the soul lesson of patience.

Exercise 42 (PE 11.1) - Assess Structure Taught

Structural Exercise 1: Take Subject-Wise Feedback

Taking feedback from parents regarding the educational design is a routine activity in schools. However, it is also necessary to take feedback from the children to find out how motivating or cumbersome they find their studies.

There are several details taught in schools which are completely irrelevant for adult life. For example, there is no need to teach children how to measure the distance of the Earth from the moon or how many battles Akbar fought. If some students want to learn science or history in detail later, they can specialize when they are older. Such details create restlessness in majority of the students. When forced to learn, their patience gets used up in trying to feel motivated.

By applying patience in learning unnecessary trivialities, children become restless in other areas which they need to focus more upon. If syllabus is kept such that it is relevant to everyday life of the students, it requires less patience to learn.

After every chapter, there needs to be some feedback questions. Each student needs to answer briefly but with patience about what he liked and disliked in the chapter. For example, you can ask:

What did you like about this chapter and the examples given? What did you dislike about this chapter and the methodology of learning used?

If several children express they found the work exercises or homework too long or unnecessarily drilling, the syllabus/methodology used for teaching/working needs to be revised over the year end or whenever possible .

Exercise 42 (PE 11.2) – Overtime Feedback from Students

Take feedback from students after every semester about every subject, extra -curricular activities and the methods of training used. Ask them what they like about the activities they enjoy and what they dislike about the activities they do not enjoy.

The activities which appear boring can be subsequently made easier, shorter or simpler so that patience is less used up and learning motivation is increased.

Maintain anonymity while taking feedback.

Exercise 43 (PE 11.3) - Feedback on Calmness acquired

*Structural Exercise 2- Take Feedback from Teachers &
Parents on Students Level of Peacefulness*

Feedback Exercise 1 – take Feedback from Teachers

The education system can largely contribute towards maintenance of peace in the world. If students are peaceful while learning, they would display good behavior at home. If students are pressurized, they would display restlessness at home.

Learning needs to be pleasurable and not performance driven in childhood. Children need to feel relaxed, excited and happy after absorbing new information. Patience will increase if children like what they study and do not feel bored.

Feedback exercise 2 - Ask Feedback from Parents:

Ask the parents to fill an anonymous form on the increase or decrease in the peacefulness of the child during the academic year.

Other factors can also be responsible for restlessness. You can ask the parents if there are any specific factors in the house which could be causing excessive unrest. If there are no disturbing or changing factors in the house, it can be presumed that the child is finding the syllabus over bearing and is releasing the frustration at home.

Modify the syllabus and test peacefulness again. Test of how education is affecting peacefulness of children needs to be a continued review assessment activity.

Structural Exercise 3- Ensure Applicability Of Syllabus in Everdyay Life With Original Thinking Over Imitative Thinking

Teaching needs to focus on making learning meaningful in everyday lives of the students than theory based or rote driven. Children need to be able to think and apply solutions originally as an outcome of the concepts taught.

Theory based learning can be frustrating and make the children robotic in thinking. Children become conditioned into obeying without thinking in schools and the same patterns continue, in adulthood.

This habit of obeying blindly creates several problems in adult lives where people prefer to obey religious traditions blindly whether the religious rituals make them more peaceful or not. Blind obedience in children creates blind faith in adults.

It is necessary to teach children how to reason, apply knowledge and change their mindsets according to circumstances. Children need to be taught to question traditions, religions, fashion trends, celebrity cult and political scenarios so that they can be prevented from getting fooled by populist leaders. Logical reasoning and application of independent thought have to be trained as mind skills.

Children who are conditioned to follow trends blindly become greedy for fame and money in adult lives. They seek approval by becoming popular even if their independent thinking gets compromised in the process of seeking popularity. Children who are aggressive subsequently may join the army, police or criminal mafia, where they blindly kill on order.

By using the conditioned doctrine of blind obedience, leaders create terrorists and criminals who kill without applying logic. The whole structure of restlessness in society can be challenged by changing the structural foundation of education such that the syllabus appears meaningful and logical to the children and they learn out of a desire to learn, not out of fear of disapproval or punishment.

Exercise 45 (PE 11.5) – Encourage logic over imitation

Exercise to Reduce Blind Imitation by Developing Logical Awareness

Motivate the students to have discussions on current fashion trends, toys, sports, religion etc. . . . . . where they feel free to express their likes and dislikes. Encourage deviation from mass conditioned thought and allow development of original thinking.

For example, if there are discussion on fashion trends and some children speak against Barbie dolls, there would be several girls who would get the option to reject Barbie as the ultimate toy to possess. However, if there are no discussions and Barbie advertises itself as the best product, the monopoly rules as there are no opposing opinions.

Similarly, the addiction for watching cricket and other sports can be questioned through discussions in schools. Popular films, TV serials and video games can be discussed with focus on dislikes so that children are made aware that everything popular is not necessarily good but only well marketed.

Children need to hear opposite perspectives from the perspective which is sold in the market.

This exercise will increase patience in children to wait and question before taking decisions. Patience will reduce anxiety to follow populist trends to be the best competitively. An ability to question popular ideals which create unrest would increase general peacefulness.

Exercise 46 (PE 11.6)- Teach Peacefulness as a subject

Structural exercise 4 - Keep Separate Time for Teaching Peacefulness as a Discipline

Peacefulness has to be trained as English or Maths are, through all the levels of schooling. Peacefulness can be trained through exercises on meditation, emotional management, yoga, breathing exercises, positive visualization and also, theoretically, by devising subject curriculum around stories of peace.

The present education system focuses more on stories of wars and victories which subconsciously motivates children to fight individualistic wars of freedom in adulthood. Instead, there is a need to train children to learn how to be peaceful in adulthood by learning lessons of forgiveness, perseverance and diligence. Everyday life is a war field for most human beings who are constantly battling between a negative mind-set and energies of optimism.

Specific training would help the positive energies win over negative energies.

The following exercises need to be taught to children to be peaceful:

Simple Meditation Exercise:

Meditation is the process of slowing down mental activity and activate a state of detachment. Simple meditation encompasses the ability to sit in complete silence and watch one vibrational movement; be it the breathing of the body or the sound of a clock ticking. Focusing on one thought slows down mind waves by taking focus away from several thoughts moving simultaneously. The focus on one vibrational movement makes the person drift into a state of feeling detached from circumstances. This detachment slowly allows the person to move into a place on inner bliss and peacefulness.

The mind cannot be kept silent as feelings are like breathing. The single minded vibrational focus on breathing /counting etc. is necessary to feel some energy movement or the body would die. The focus of teaching meditation needs to be on developing the ZERO state, to facilitate upliftment of subconscious energies from staying negative/ stressed.

The vibrations of energy movement follow three vibrational states of Mind: the negative mind-set, the Zero/neutral /detached mind-set and the positive mind-set. The ZERO State is also called a BRAKE/GAP State as it metaphorically represents a BRAKE function. Just as car needs to be put on neutral gear for reversing, the mind needs to be put on a neutral state of detachment for reversing the direction of the mind from negative to positive.

Happiness is a positive vibration and can be obtained as a routine vibrational energy only after developing ZERO states of mind. The ZERO state takes the focus away from the negative state of mind and helps the body's energies rise to a positive vibration.

Ideally, simple meditation on being in a detached state of mind needs to be done for ten minutes daily, where a neutral state of mind can be alternated with positive imagination so that the mind does not dip into the negative state of worrying at any point during these ten minutes. One minute meditation in every hour is also good .

Exercise 47 (PE 11.7) – Stepwise Meditation

Technique of Meditation:

1. Sit or lie down with spinal cord/ back straight.
2. Try to keep your eyes rolled up to prevent negative thinking.

3. Start focusing on breathing at any one point of the body. It helps to focus on the area underneath the nostrils or on the stomach while breathing in and out.

4. If the mind starts getting bored and tries to run away, move deliberately to a positive imagination where you are peaceful.

5. Focus on Deliberately creating feelings of patience and peacefulness.

6. After a few seconds of feeling peaceful/ happy/ successful in your imagination, move back to the detached state.

7. Do not focus on any negative thinking, worries or How's during these allotted minutes.

8. Ask the mind to bring up worries later after you allotted meditation time is up. Mind obeys.

9. It is easier to concentrate if you keep an alarm clock for one / two or five/ten minutes. After ten minutes are over, end the meditation with a smile.

10. Thank Earth and the Creator for a wonderful life and be peaceful while doing any task.

Try to not focus on worrying for another ten minutes though mind will start bringing up worries after the allotted time. Postpone negative thinking as long as is possible. A focus on inner silence brings up several underlying problems which may have to be subsequently healed through Emotional Management techniques.

Be aware that though the above exercise is good for adults, focusing only on silence for ten minutes may not be possible for children.

If ten minutes is difficult to assign, the school can allot time to focus on silence for two minutes at least. For routine development of peacefulness, focusing on silence for two minutes for about five times a day is also good. The ten minutes can be divided into five slots.

Two minutes per day for five days a week can be allotted for developing peacefulness and patience in the routine schedule. THE TWO MINUTE Silence time integrated with meditation exercises, as given below, can be incorporated during different periods like the yoga class, prayer time, tiffin time , dance class, sports etc.

Five Different Methods of Two minutes Meditation

The following two-minutes meditation exercises can be used like computer programs to instill peacefulness in the mind which would improve concentration, focus, positive thinking and patience simultaneously.

Exercise 48 (PE 11.8) – Practice Meditation for one minute – twp minutes

Meditation Exercise 1: Simple Breathing

As the students to sit straight and focus on breathing in their stomach. Let their eyes look upwards and a SMILE come on their face. Looking upwards will prevent the mind from random thinking.

Then just allow them to feel their stomach move in and out

while SMILING.

2 - Meditation through Deep Breathing Exercises

Calmness can also be created through training the students in deep breathing exercises.

Method for Two Minute Calming Breath exercise:

1. Ask the students to take a long breath in to the count of 5.
2. Hold the breath to the count of 5
3. Exhale slowly to the count of 5.
4. Then, be silent for five seconds.
5. Repeat the exercise five times.

The count can be modified, as required.

For two minutes of breathing calmness, ask the children to do the breathing exercise five times , then maintain silence for thirty seconds and again do the breathing exercise for five times and again maintain silence for thirty seconds .

Exercise 50 (PE 11.10) - Combining Body movement and Meditative Silence

Meditation through Physical Exercise:

All physical exercises need to be combined with meditation .After ten minutes of rigorous physical exercise, two minutes of complete silence needs to be maintained before the body can be set free to loosen up.

Mediation exercise 3 - Two Minutes Physical Exercise with Calming Meditation

1. Ask the children to raise up their hands
2. Hold for five seconds
3. Join the hands together above the head
4. Hold for five seconds
5. Separate hands and hold for five seconds
6. Bring down the hands with the count of 5.
7. Maintain silence for fifteen seconds
8. Repeat the exercise two times.
9. Maintain silence for about thirty seconds at the end of the exercise.

Exercise 51 (PE 11.11)- Practice Mechanical Visualization, 2 minutes

Meditation exercise 4 - Calming Visualization Exercise for Two minutes

For the younger students, combine visualization with manifestation.

Ask the smaller students to think that they are eating a sweet for thirty seconds.

After thirty seconds, give them a sweet.
Then, ask them to again be in the memory of eating the sweet.

You can replace the sweet with any imaginative idea.

Older students can visualize without physical aids. You can ask the older students to imagine the above given physical exercise without real hand movements. The visualization will help them understand their subconscious neural circuitry.

Do the following exercise with no physical movement involved. This is a purely imaginative exercise. Any other movements can also be imagined.

1. Ask the students to imagine raising up their hands. Hold for five seconds.
2. Ask them to imagine joining the hands together. Hold for five seconds.
3. Ask the students to imagine bringing down the hands. Hold for five seconds.
4. Ask the students to wait for five seconds.
5. Again ask them to imagine raising their hands up, holding them together and bringing them down.
6. Wait for thirty seconds with a SMILE. The no-action waiting time of a few seconds interval will bring a peaceful state of mind for long.

You will realize that the mind waves move the same way in an imagined activity as in a real activity. This simple exercise proves that the neural circuitry of the subconscious mind gets activated during an imagined activity as in a physical activity.

This is an important exercise for controlling the subconscious mind. Just as mind waves move in imagination during this physical exercise, mind waves move during thinking of worries & accidents as much as they do when real problems come up. All real problems are created by manifestation of the mind focusing upon those problems as feelings, subconsciously through focusing on bad memories of the past, other people's problems or fears of accidents in the future.
Imagination with feelings releases negative hormones in the body and negative expectations as electric wave circles which impact future reality. These concepts are explained in more detail in my other book, CREATION OF HAPPINESS: THE ENERGY WAR, a Soul's Perspective and A COURSE IN EMOTIONAL MANAGEMENT

Exercise 52 (PE 11.12)- Practice Creative Visualization, 2 minutes

Meditation exercise 5 - Two Minutes Calming Meditation with Positive Creative Visualization

The following exercise has been created for peacefulness but the same technique can be used to manifest any feeling desired

Patience is necessary to prevent feelings of helplessness. Helplessness arises when you cannot control your sad feelings. To get control in life, you need to be able to co-create the feelings you desire. Creation of reality depends on how you expect it to be. What you imagine today may manifest six days later or six years later but if you do not imagine anything, other people's thinking will dominate your mind and your reality will be an expectation of what they thought for you, whether you like it or not .

Training children to imagine their own future helps them get in control of their feelings/ subconscious vibrational movement, which affects future manifestations.

A two minute exercise on imagining would help in activating the imaginative mind of the child. These exercises can extend for longer duration.

Since peacefulness is the most needed energy in today's world, it would help society if children started imagining being peaceful for creating peacefulness in their future. Being peaceful improves health and concentration.

Whatever is imagined with intensity becomes a repertoire for future action plan. Imagining peacefulness with activation of all sense organs would ensure that the feelings imagined manifest overtime.

Calming Positive Visualization for Manifesting Peacefulness

Ask the kindergarten children to be peaceful for two -

thirty seconds four times a day. If possible, show them pictures of peaceful children and ask them to sit or smile the same way.

The older children can be asked to imagine how it would be peaceful or have a peaceful life.
Most of us desire peace but never have the patience to sit back and imagine a peaceful life. Till we create the feelings in our mind, the feelings cannot be created in our external lives. Hence, it would significantly help if children are trained into creating peacefulness by imagining how it would be to be stress free, happy, healthy and peaceful.

Steps for Visualization Exercise for Being Peaceful

During these period pf visualization, ask the children to be totally in the film they create and not focus on any problems. Focusing on problems will block manifestation of peaceful feelings by creating feelings of helplessness. To reduce helplessness in routine life, it is necessary to focus clearly on energies of peacefulness mentally even for short durations.

Do not focus on the HOWs or Whys or any reasons on why this scenario is not happening currently. The current picture of your life is an outcome of a past visualization. To create a different future, create a different focus in the present without any obstructions coming in the mind space.

You may use the following words:

"Imagine how it would be to be peaceful and happy. Imagine your house when you feel peaceful. Imagine the sounds you hear, the pictures you see, the smells you have, the tastes you feel in your mouth, the touch of fabric/ furniture around you, the calm feelings you have in your body etc. Smile in thankfulness that you are peaceful and healthy.

Imagine how it would be to be peaceful/without tension in school / any activity area. How does it feel to work/play/dance/ sing in peace? What are the pictures you see, the sounds you hear, the smells around you, the tastes and touch of working in peace, the feelings of having less/ no obstructions and working in contentment. Also imagine the feelings of being acknowledged and acknowledging the self.

Imagine how it would be if the planet Earth was in peace? Imagine the feelings of people around you. Imagine the smiles, the sounds of relaxation, the atmosphere of contentment, the smell of cleanliness, the taste of healthy food, the touch of clean atmosphere. Activate all these sensory inputs and smile in gratitude that you are living on a content and peaceful Earth.

Ask the children to talk about or write their observations.

Caution - Make sure that the children remain optimistic

or detached during or after this visualization exercise and do not become negative by worrying about the How's. Only focus on activating clear, positive energy channels without any focus on negative feelings. Try not to create any discussion on problems for atleast ten minutes after the exercise is over.

Doing these exercise will increase patience in children automatically as they would spend some time being away from problems. The positive feelings would break automated negative energy circuits in the mind with deliberate forcefulness. Feelings of detachment will open clustered negative energy threads and create space for new feelings to come in.

The time and space for these exercises can be modified according to individual requirements.

Exercise 53 (PE 11.13) – Development Of Flexibility

Structural Change Exercise 5: Start the day Late, Reduce Pressure of School Timings

Schools have been running like armies to ensure mass obedience. However, the same principle of obedience creates terrorists, assassins and alcoholics who are so bound by the obedience cult that they do not use original thinking to defend their own conscience. Hence, children have to be taught to disobey with discipline, break rules and voice their opinions to enable evolution of consciousness to a higher positive dimension.

It is the norm to start the day early in today's modern world. Everybody is pressurized and running to meet targets. However, this created anxiety overtime becomes a habit of the mind and the reason for increasing frustration in society, discontentment, restlessness, anger and violence.

Anxiety has to be reduced by choice to decondition the mind from feeling pressured.

Exercise Getting Up Late. Even if your eyes open, stay in bed in silence and try to meditate. Make your sleep timings flexible. Allow your body clock to shift itself and relax with the shifts. Reschedule your work. Allow the robotic mind-set to break with gaps in thinking so that the mind is forced to think differently.

You will be less angry if you rest more and overtime, be more creative. Happiness and peacefulness rises if your day starts feeling rested in your own space.

The following explanation is given for this radical approach to breaking mind-sets:

Getting up early is traditionally considered good training for survival. However, traditional thinking is based on stereotyped thinking carried over from the primitive perspective of survival. Early morning was useful for the kind of schedule which primitive man used when no work could be done after sunset.

However , in today's word, there does not need to be stress on early mornings, as electricity is available and work can be done at nights as much as in the mornings. It was presumed that mornings are good for working in earlier times because the mind is fresh in the morning but in the modern world, the mind is stressed in the morning and no longer fresh as most people like to stay awake with electricity on. People like to use the night time for private work which could not be done in the hustle-bustle of the day. Several parents who come home late like to spend the night time with their children which they have to sacrifice to force the kids to sleep early to get up for school. The pressure of sleeping early and getting up early causes stress to several parents and children.

Also, creative people are known to prefer working late at nights which prevents them from keeping an early morning schedule .From the perspective of optimum brain rejuvenation also, early morning time is the best time for sleeping peacefully . Early morning sleep is supposed to be the most restful.

Early mornings is also the best time for meditation as it gives free space away from a crowd of voices and thoughts which camouflage clear thinking during the day , whether you are sleeping in bed or walking alone in free space . Everybody does not have problems in getting up early in the morning but several people have severe problems due to an early morning schedule, which can be avoided simply by allowing them to get up later and more relaxed.

Early morning mind-set is very rigid in today's world. However, the habit has to be broken because forcing oneself to get up from deep sleep is the reason for people feeling forced through life in every job they undertake. Feelings repeat themselves and the feeling you get up with sets the tone of the day. If you get up feeling compromised, you live feeling compromised. If you get up feeling relaxed, life appears to be a relaxing journey.

Incomplete rest during sleep is a big reason for headaches during the day, irritability in temperaments, inability to sleep peacefully at night, need for alcohol and drugs to relax, inability to focus on creative tasks, food indigestions, diseases which get created by a focus on worrying, release of stress- related negative hormones in the body and several aggression problems of society which are a result of feeling like slaves at work.

The violence which boys exhibit can be reduced substantially by allowing them to get up late, feeling peaceful and relaxed. The mind has to be conditioned into resting peacefully in the morning for it to remain peaceful and focused as a habit during the day.

The early morning drill makes the body feel like a running machine which suppresses peacefulness of the soul, thus reducing happiness. In semi drowsy states, the mind gets conditioned, mechanically into focusing on the first feeling it gets into repeatedly. Getting up feeling angry and grumpy creates a negative thinking cycle which keeps rotating around a point of negative focus automatically, and external circumstances are created such that this negative focus remains maintained (By the Law of Vibrations)

A life-long cycle of stress and resentment starts because children are forced to get up when they can be trained into feeling peaceful as an energy cycle, by allowing them to get up naturally later. The restlessness is forced by making children get up to work when they can be allowed to sleep in a natural state of resting.

Training children like oxen for work or donkeys to slave creates clerks in thinking who obey orders more easily than taking independent, responsible decisions.

Changing school timings to start at around 10 am would give parents, teachers, staff and children more time to relax and finish early morning chores before rushing to school.

10 am to 4 pm will ensure that same school timings remain .If 10 am is too late, schools can start with timings of 9 am to 3 pm , given that six hours is the compulsory shift .

Further research needs to be done on reducing the school duration to find how many hours are needed for optimum quality performance over focus on quantitative results.

Ideally, six hours of schooling is not needed. Children get very tired in a six hourly schedule .Adults work for eight hour shifts. Schools can work at four or five hour schedules for more quality work. Long school timings produce more quantity work than quality improvement in intelligence.

 A school which starts at 10 am can close at 3 pm and a school which starts at 9 am can close at 2 pm. less number of hours would motivate children to give more concentration to the hours they work.

These timings need not necessarily apply to schools which have a morning shift and an afternoon shift .However , most public schools have a single shift and can afford to make the shift in schedule to start later in the day .

Five days school routine is better than a six days school routine. A four day school routine is also advisable, where a day in between the week can be kept off. A holiday in between will keep spirits motivated through the week and will reduce grumbling and self -pity further with not much reduction in quality of education.

Quality of education cannot be measured by quantity of syllabus taught or number of hours put into school. Several children who excel in life are drop outs from school because school discipline curbs creative thinking

Quality of education and understanding of the mind requires patience. Increasing patience in life requires a choice to be peaceful by making changes in life-style which are creating harassment.

New methods of focus which improve quality of education imparted would help to evolve consciousness towards a more peaceful existence.

Chapter 12 - Exercises to Increase Positive Thinking, Confidence & Responsibility

Children have to be trained into responsibility to become responsible adults. Training children to become positive thinkers, self -confident, patient and responsible would increase their answerability to society when they grow up.

Several people earn money and fame without caring about the impact of their work on mass consciousness. If their work spreads more unhappiness than happiness in the lives of others, the overall positive energy on the planet reduces; thus increasing problems in society for everyone.

Energy transfer happens through feelings experienced during actions and thoughts of each individual. If each individual was given a sense of responsibility to spread positive energy such that it increases happiness, health and peacefulness in society in small or big ways; it would increase the individual's self-worth, and positive energy, health and happiness would increase for all.

Children have to be trained into a pattern of working that it increases happiness for self while increasing positive contribution to others. At present, in a competitive structure, happiness for self is targeted such that it reduces happiness of others. When you defeat others and win yourself or mock others to feel yourself as superior, you increase bitterness in the atmosphere which may lead to aggressive conflicts , increase in violence and sadness in the minds of several, that reduces overall peace and balance .

 The following ways can be used to reduce negative thinking and increase positive thinking in students:

Exercise 54 (PE 12.1) – Increase self confidence

Make the children write five good things about themselves every day, so that they notice the positive aspects of their individuality.

Every person is born with some good qualities and some errors/ negative qualities.

Next, ask them to write two negative things about themselves so that they also notice the errors. Ask them how the errors help them stay balanced. Also, find out if they are comfortable with the errors or they would be better if the errors were removed.

Every negative feeling helps in some way. Every difficulty has a positive intention attached to it which can be deciphered to change the problem into a positive learning experience. No human being can be perfect as a human body is created by mixing pure energies of spirit with dense solid matter which is negative in atomic structure.

The mistakes in the person help the person stay balanced in his own way. For example, if a person likes playing and does not like studying, low concentration in studies can help him excel at sports and stay away from academic pressure.

Children who like painting , dancing or singing may not be as good at academics because the soul wants to choose its area of excellence and focus on that instead of splitting energy equally in all parts of life .

Similarly, if a child is academically oriented, s/he may be less interested in sports or other activities. If a child likes only to read, she maybe clumsy in other organizing work.

The difficulty helps the child focus on areas of excellence and defocus on areas of deficiency.

 Self -confidence of the child would increase if the difficulties are accepted without negative judgement being attached to the area of deficiency; while the skill areas of the child are praised and allowed to increase as much as time permits.

It is often said in layman terms *"You cannot judge a fish by its ability to climb a tree "*

Asking each child to focus on five or ten good aspects of self daily, would tremendously help in increasing self-confidence. A positive self- confidence would increase a sense of responsibility towards the world in which s/he lives as a more positive world would make him happier in the long run.

Exercise 55 (PE 12.2) - Increase Positive Focus

Ask the children to:

Find five - ten good things which they like about their school / work area.

Find five - ten good things which they like about their friends/ teachers/ staff/ home/ parents/ siblings etc.

Since the focus is external here and not on self, it is not necessary to focus on the negative aspects of these situations, as change would not be possible unless there is mutual/ collective consensus. However, just focusing on the positive aspects of school and people around would make the children happier and more confident about the environment they work in.

Deliberately focusing on positive aspects in the environment is necessary to feel good about the self and the world.

Happiness, self- worth and a desire to be responsible rise automatically by focusing on positive feelings. Counting ten good things in your environment every day increases the positive feeling that you are living in a good environment and your life situation is helping you become wiser/ stronger/ resilient.

It also trains the children to find the positive in every aspect of life when they grow up. If you move in life with a focus on finding the blessings attached to every difficult situation, you would feel more confident and overcome the negative energy sooner but if you are bent upon expecting the worst in every situation, you would slowly deteriorate in terms of health, happiness and peace.

It is natural for the subconscious mind to focus more on negative aspects than on positive aspects of a situation. The subconscious mind is trained from the primitive man's mind-set to look around for threat and danger every five seconds.

Hence, the mind has to be deliberately trained to focus away from the negative aspects of a situation to focus on the positive aspects of the same situation.

Some people become so conditioned into being negative that they think there is nothing positive in their life. However, with persistent training and practice, the focus can be shifted to finding positive aspects of every situation.

Exercise 56 (PE 12.3) – Practice Patience, Teach Delaying Gratification

Delaying gratification by ten seconds before taking action helps significantly in lowering tempers in adult lives. Training in developing patience & peacefulness has to be given from childhood.

1. While answering questions in excitement, ask the child who is selected to hold his/her breath for ten seconds before giving a response. The response would be less excitable and more methodical. If not, again ask him to wait till he slows down and thinks out the response

instead of just answering it by rote.

2. While going for lunch, ask the children to drink a glass of water before eating. The water will help digestion and delay eating in a hurry.

3. While sitting for lunch, ask the children to visualize contentment for ten seconds and thank the universe/ God before eating, as mentioned in chapter 9.

4. While resolving mutual anger based conflicts, ask the children to wait for ten seconds before complaining. This will reduce the need to self-defend or blame, excessively. Heated reactions of anger considerably reduce if a ten seconds gap is trained in between the mental feeling aroused and the oral reaction. The delay of response calms down the person to react calmly than as a trigger pulled by another.

5. At the end of each chapter, ask the children to wait for ten seconds and absorb the knowledge before closing their books.

Children have to be trained in response behaviors for the mind to be conditioned into delaying gratification.

Delaying gratification is one of the most important skills for learning patience and reducing aggressive behavior in adult lives.

Often anger come when work is not done on time or according to desired expectations. However, delaying gratification for ten seconds allows the brain to let go of intense tension and release stress enough to view the situation peacefully without negative personal judgement involved.

Exercise 57 (PE 12.4) - Visualize Completion

Teach Visualization of Completion with Feeling Happy

Any work can be done more effectively if it is visualized as complete along with increase in inner happiness, before it is attempted.

Children have to be mentally trained to visualize the feelings of completion of a task, by using abstract imagination with patience before taking action.

Abstract imagination is similar to day dreaming. The main difference between day-dreaming and created visualization is that the visualization has a goal of achievement wherein day dreaming can be aimless. Visualization focuses on creating feelings of happiness in the brain which helps in generating positive hormones with deliberate awareness whereas day dreaming can make you slip into negativity anytime without awareness.

Visualization helps in obtaining desired results with more precision in any activity of life – be it a school project or an adult work relationship. The desired feelings start to manifest during the course of progress. Without setting an aim for feelings desired through an outcome, the work effort can result in sad/restless feelings, and may create distress more than the happiness envisaged, due to energy wasted in trial and error procedures.

If there is no visualization of the desired completed positive feelings, trial and error to create happiness from effort, takes longer. There is a greater desire to give up, in between, than make an effort to complete a task. Also, the outcome achieved may not lead to inner happiness, thus leading to disappointment in children, which creates frustration with doing effort, subsequently.

If children are trained into mentally creating the effort of completing a task and achieving desired results with increasing happiness, the outcome would be such that it would make the children more positive than negative.

For example, if a student who gets 50 % in an exam, visualizes a test result as 100 %, it may manifest as 70 % on the physical realm as doubts and other obstructions would block the complete visualization from manifesting. However, the visualizing exercise would ensure that effort is directed on the right path and 70 % of the outcome expected is manifested which would be greater than the usual result manifested.

The visualization exercise can be done while studying a chapter and before giving the exam.

Visualizations of a number of outcomes can also be trained to encourage choices of response. Visualization also helps in decision making. It is easier to take a decision if you play out the complete film in your mind of the choices you have, and choose the outcome which gives you the most desired/ satisfied feeling.

Exercise of Basic Visualization

While teaching a chapter, ask the children to close their eyes for ten seconds and visualize taking in the learning. They can take in the learning as an energy, or as a metaphor. The learning can be given a visual metaphor like a triangle/ square/ oval picture and a color, a hearing input like a buzzing sound in the mind or a musical tone etc. , a touch, a feel, a taste and a smell .

Using all sensory organs would make the learning complete in the subconscious mind which understands learning through symbols or energy intake. Words are nor directly processed by the subconscious mind but are converted into energy symbols or digits and then absorbed.

The children can also be asked to write in one sentence what they liked about the chapter to integrate the subconscious learning with the conscious mind.

Combining abstract thinking and rational thinking will increase patience and allow development of perspective.

Exercise 58 (PE 12.5) -Advanced Visualization

It has been researched that using hypnotherapy visualization helps in getting good performance results in academics and sports. A simpler method of visualization can be used for developing positive expectations as a daily routine.

Any visualization exercise requires use of all five sense organs. Ask the children to mentally create a film with the following ingredients:

Think of how it would be get the grades that you want in your report card. Give it a clear, big picture; hear what your friends/teachers/ parents say ; feel the report card in your hands as if you are looking at it now; imagine yourself eating with more pleasure after having the good report card ; imagine yourself sleeping with more confidence after having the good report card

 Or

Before giving a test, the children can be made to visualize a positive outcome. Ask them to imagine feeling happy / content with their efforts after the test results are announced.

If the visualization creates anxiety, the children can be allowed to revise if there is a need just before giving the test or they can be told that they need to focus on the feeling of happiness or being non- negative, with whatever grades they achieve. Initially, fake happiness maybe created by using detachment, where test results are not good but overtime, genuine happiness starts coming in because it has been visualized. Overtime, the children would start learning better and performing better because the subconscious mind would tune it to higher understanding.

The exercise given above can be applied to any area of life where a positive outcome is desired. For example, you can imagine feeling contentment while drawing a painting, performing in dance or having a party with friends. It is always safer to visualize contentment to organize the subconscious mind than leave the outcome to chance.

Exercise 59 (PE 12.6) – Self Motivation

Teach Rewarding the Self on Achievement

Acknowledgement increases motivation. Children work for praise and positive reinforcement. Adults work for money and success, which are metaphors of positive reinforcement, given by society.

However, depending on external motivation is not enough to be able to think positively during an ongoing activity. Often, external motivation comes after completion of a task and for activities which require exceptional endeavor in socially acceptable ways.

Self -motivation is necessary to continue effort towards a goal in good spirits. Rewarding the self is a skill which has to be taught to children so that they do not depend excessively on external approval.

Methods of Self-Motivation:

1. Do not wait for a task to be competed. Reward the

ongoing process with a pat on your own back, a smile of appreciation for yourself and a mind which tells you that you are on the right track. Keep reviewing your work, correcting the errors and motivating yourself with self acknowledgement for the effort you put in for feeling peaceful, successful or for a Higher Good.

2. The upper corner of the eye near the nose has a neurological circuit connected to self-acknowledgement in the brain. Touching yourself in the upper corner of the eye for two seconds, just under the eyebrow with a smile, is self -motivating. Teach the children that they need to feel good about a task they are doing for being self-motivated. Say "you can touch yourself on the upper corner of the eye, smile and say *well done* to yourself!"

3. Talk to yourself in second person as if a Higher Self of your own soul is talking to you. Feel your work as positive energy and appreciate it mentally. For example, say silently to yourself "Wow! Your work is complete .Good job , own name "

4. Respect your own work as an observer. Find good qualities in your own work and enumerate them loudly in your own mind. Review and acknowledge your own work as good, from an observer's perspective. For example, when you write an essay, tell yourself "Reading this essay gives me so much peace of mind. It is written with so much clarity "; "Thank God, I finished this exercise on Time. I have contentment that I finished my targeted goal for today "

These five techniques of developing patience and peacefulness can be integrated in the daily routine to increase positive thinking in children so that the automatically focus on being positive as adults.

The five exercises in this chapter , in brief were:

1. Focus on Five good things about self
2. Focus on five good things in the school/ work environment
3. Delay Gratification
4. Dream/ Visualize Completion
5. Acknowledge self progress

While focusing on teaching how to be positive as a routine, it is equally necessary to teach how not to be negative. The following chapter focuses on aspects of teaching which are normally ignored as irrelevant but which create negative behaviors, if unchecked.

Chapter 13- Teaching What Not To Do To BE Positive

Positive health and peace are a cumulative result of staying happy over a period of time by a choice to not be negative.

Children are trained into becoming negative by society. We become negative habitually are taught to focus on all the bad things happening in our lives and around us so that we can improve those situations.

However, very often, we are helpless over circumstances and do nothing on an individual level to change the negative scenario in our environment or in the world. When nothing can be done to change an external situation, it is necessary to develop detachment from it than go on worrying about it and absorbing in the negative energy of sadness.

For example, you may feel very distressed about poverty in the world but may not be able to do anything much to eradicate poverty. In that case, you need to focus on worrying about poverty and think about it if and only as much as you can help. If you cannot help due to your circumstances, you need to detach from the negative vibrations of poverty and rise to feeling positive vibrationally.

You cannot help the world by being dark yourself but you can contribute to increasing happiness in the world by being positive yourself through creating a chain of positive impulses which have a cumulative effect on the world.

While teaching children how to be positive, it is essential to teach them how not to be negative.

The following criteria need to be noted while teaching children how to work and think so that they do not behave negatively or think negatively, if it can be avoided by simple instructions.

Exercise 60 (PE 13.1) – What not to do to Concentrate better

Do not over-stress. If you over-stress, you will lose motivation. Any activity needs to be done only as much as it is not forced. Take a thirty seconds break whenever motivation decreases and restart your work. Take a longer break when you feel your concentration dropping off.

Concentration increases overtime by using mental exercises. The most easily applied exercise is a simple focus on silence. **Start with a single point focus for thirty seconds. You may focus on your navel point or the area under your nostrils or on your crown chakra at the top of the pineal gland or on your feet. You may choose any point of focus where you feel most relaxed & least distracted, while focusing.**

Time with an alarm clock. Do not exercise arbitrarily as the mind will not focus with all its strength if no clear finishing line is given.

Exercise 61 (PE 13.2) – What not to do to study/focus better

Avoid participating in distractions like chatting with friends, watching television etc. even if it is going on the side while you are studying . . . Do not strain all your sense organs at the same time. Detachment from enjoyable, glittering, ritualistic activities is necessary to find peace in your inner self. Your desire to study or focus on a creative task would be less if there are too many sounds or exciting visions around. Try to move to a silent place for studying, obtaining inner peacefulness and meditation.

However, if there are distractions which pull you, and you should concentrate on your inner self for studying or meditation or painting etc. . . . . . ; You need to learn how to detach with force. Detachment often requires more skill and effort than concentrating.

Obtaining a ZERO state of mind is necessary to move to a positive state of mind from a negative state of mind. ZERO frequency of mental vibrations lies between a restless state and a focused state of mind.

Detachment is a ZERO state of mind, where you choose not to get involved with others' problems to focus on yourself and raising your inner positive frequency from restlessness to centeredness. The following technique would help in detachment:

Create imagined walls around your ears so that the sound from others does not distract you.

You can create imagined walls by meditating in silence with focus on your ears. Keep your hands up, elbows parallel to the ground and palms adjacent to the height of your ears. This posture blocks thought waves from entering and relaxed the soul. While meditating, you can imagine walls around the ears on both sides ...

In your meditation, you are connected to your subconscious mind. Mentally, ask the walls to insulate you from distracting noises. You can also ask the walls to stay as long as commanded and to dissolve only when told. You can also ask the walls to re-activate whenever commanded silently. Meditate for thirty seconds every morning in silence and before sleeping at night to make these silencing walls a part of your repertoire.

Exercise 62 (PE 13.3) - What not to do while preparing for a goal?

Focus more on the feelings desired than the physical acknowledgement you seek.

Get in the space of BEING more than doing and having.

A focus on only getting acknowledgment in the physical world will distract you from getting inner satisfaction along with the outer goal you seek to attain .

For example, if you want to be selected to dance in a school performance, focus on why you want to be selected. When you focus on the **why,** you will not feel disappointed if you are not selected and you will be able to work with more enjoyment when you are selected.

When you seek a goal, you always have a feeling which you desire BEING while in that role. For example, if you want to go to a picnic with your friends, you want to be a fun loving person who is relaxed and cheerful. Similarly, if you seek a relationship with a person of the opposite sex, you want to be that person who is loved and admired.

Often, in adult lives, it is found that the external goal is achieved without the feeling desired attained. For example, you may go to a picnic and feel lonely or you may attract a relationship but feel more criticized than loved. Your craving for the feeling you seek to attain continues till the BEING is satisfied.

Hence, while desiring a goal, it is better to focus on the feeling you desire to BE than on the desired picture .The picture of success is meaningless if the inner feelings are not attained.

It takes longer to attain inner satisfaction with external effort but the waiting is worth the effort than attaining success with feeling dis-satisfied.

Exercise 64 (PE 13.4) - What not to do while in a task driven atmosphere?

Do not become a slave of others in your mind. Be careful that you do not acquire a slave mentality where you keep obeying without thinking in fear of punishment or argument. Always remember that your first task is to evolve your own consciousness to a higher level of inner satisfaction, peace & happiness.

In today's world, there is a tendency to push around. Everybody wants you to work for goals designed by a super-structure. However, you may not agree with all these task driven strategies and may do several tasks half-heartedly because you are trained into obedience ...

To avoid becoming a slave of other's thinking, take time off to meditate for a few seconds every hour. Take ten seconds out for yourself with awareness, whenever you can.

Roll your eyes up and smile while feeling the energy in your stomach during these ten seconds.

This habit of breaking from routine will prevent another's mind from dominating over yours. You will be able to detach yourself automatically from obeying orders blindly. Detachment will help you decide what your goals are and why they are different from another's goals.

Work with focus is possible only if the feelings you desire as satisfaction are the same as the feelings desired by the other in authority.

If the person in authority is confused, anxious or biased by religion/ traditions/ old rules etc... , then the feelings desired would not lead to optimum satisfaction for anybody who is involved. You will suffer as everybody else if you obey blindly a structure which is creating more dissatisfaction and disharmony than peace because of rigidity involved in its thinking.

To be able to think with clarity, do not allow invasion of strong negative energy which comes on as a wind with force. Insulate yourself by keeping walls on ears or filter out the words from the strong, assertive tone by focusing away from the sound with detachment.

For example, whenever another person scolds you or abuses

you, take your mind away from his words for ten seconds and look up into the sky. Then, try to be in the sky and gauge the situation from an observer's perspective. That will help you decide whether the person abusing is correct and you could obey and whether the other person is being unjust or negative by temperament and you could disobey, as well. If you keep taking ten seconds off, to be silent inside your mind, you will detach automatically. With detachment, you will not be forced to obey under pressure of a public image.

Also, if you have to obey even if you disagree, detach from negative feelings and do the task mechanically so that it does not become a part of your repertoire. Detachment develops if you react after a gap.

For example, before choosing to feel sad or angry about a situation, take ten seconds off. Delay your inner reaction by ten seconds. The ten seconds break will remove the steam of emotions rising onside you and you will be able to react to the situation from a calmer perspective.

Do not allow the atmosphere to rule you so much that you become a slave to your own reactions to another's pressurizing attitude. Often, you may become controlled by other people's dominating energies if you do not learn to detach automatically with practiced mind training.

Taking the ten seconds break several time s a day from all thinking activity, will allow you to choose positive feelings over negative; and leave activities which make you feel non-intelligent or dis-respected.

Do not exercise or dance continuously without taking a break to rest.

Heavy exercise or dancing will create a hormonal imbalance in your body to burn your stamina. Your heart - rate, blood pressure, adrenalin flow etc. will rise during the exercising activity.

However, if you do not regulate this rising hormonal discharge, it will suddenly clamp down and make you depressed or lethargic. The hormonal balance needs to be balanced deliberately by combining exercises and dancing with meditation/ maintaining silence in the inner self.

Also, meditating with awareness during exercises helps to reduce weight more effectively than continuous, harsh exercises. Slow breathing exercises combined with silent meditation help the blood flow to the brain thus improving concentration and mental skills like intelligence, problem solving etc.

As a routine, give a break of two minutes after ten minutes of fast exercise. Give one third or one fifth of the exercising time for being in silence in your mind with focus on your breath going in and out. Try to keep your eyes rolled up and smile inside during the meditation time so that your mind does not escape into brooding or worrying.

Smiling will release positive hormones in the body which will make you feel fresh during the exercise.

Exercise 66 (PE 13.6) -What not to do while Having Fun?

While each person likes to relax by having fun, the element of relaxation often go missing from the activities which constitute fun.

Do not have fun by becoming addictive to it. The element of detachment is critical while having fun. Fun is that which is not compulsive.

If the need for fun becomes compulsive, it becomes an addiction and makes you lose self-control.

Fun is relaxing when you can leave the act of having fun anytime without feeling sad or depressed. The relaxation obtained during the fun activity helps you be positive, if the relaxation continues after you leave the fun creating activity.

If you feel addicted to the increase of adrenaline flow, then the fun creating activity may become harmful to your inner hormonal state of balance.

Therefore, fun should be indulged in with breaks to detach from its addictive/unbalancing element. For example if you have fun while watching cricket, you should not allow yourself to get over-excited or depressed if someone else loses or wins a game .

Similarly, if you have fun while drinking alcohol, the after effects of alcohol should not depress you more than the positive effects of drinking alcohol. For example, the hangover should not create headaches the next day such that you feel helpless over your body and your circumstances.

Likewise, if you are above 15 years of age, your fun should not be such that it creates sexual imbalances in you which create lust in you over the need to be loved. For example, if you have fun while dancing all night, your root chakra at the base of your spine and sexual chakra may lose balance and you may feel the need to continue dancing or take drugs or have sex to calm yourself down. The craving after the activity is over maybe more than the pleasure you feel while the activity is going on.

You cannot continue to have body fun non-stop as it would divert you from other areas of interest which give you more inner satisfaction. Your positive soul frequency would rise and increase your happiness and health only if you attain peacefulness with the work you do.

Having fun may relax you but it needs it be indulged only as long as any physical exercise is needed? Just as exercising cannot become your only interest in life, as that would make you robotic; having fun cannot become your only interest in life as that would make you ape-like in problem solving.

People who escape into fun whenever any problem arises, do not develop higher intelligence and remain in the same patterns of emotional problems throughout life.

While fun and exercise are as needed as eating and sleeping, an addiction to fun prevents development of intelligence needed to evolve to a higher level of happiness and health consciousness.

Exercise 6.7 (PE – 13.7) - What not to do while making plans of success?

Do not make plans of success which have no element of inner happiness entailed.

For example, if you make plans of success where you earn lots of money, ensure that you also have planned ways by which this money would increase your emotional well- being , improve your health and satisfaction with your circumstances .

Usually, earning money by itself does not improve emotional satisfaction or health. People who spend their lives earning money keep craving for more in the same way as people keep craving for more fun. Earning money for itself or for buying products, becomes an addiction which leaves you feeling empty and deprived of love.

Success needs to be planned so that you feel more love

for yourself, more gratitude towards God and more appreciation for all those who help you because your happiness and peace rise with the efforts you make.

The road to success which includes happiness and not money as the criteria is longer but there is contentment along the way.

The road to success which gets you money is shorter but there are feelings of meaninglessness along the way.

The evolution from earning money as a means of success to earning happiness is the same as the evolution of humans from being animals.

Earning money is being animal-like in orientation while increasing levels of happiness are possible only with evolution of intelligence.

Evolution takes longer than survival. For example, an animal kid walks faster but does not develop in intelligence, whereas a human kid takes much longer to walk but evolves in intelligence simultaneously. Similarly, the animal mind-set of a human being makes him kill and lust for money but does not find contentment ever; whereas a human being aiming at satisfaction takes longer to find the correct route but maintains good health and inner clarity with the means pursued.

Therefore, while making goals for success, make simultaneous plans for the feelings of emotional satisfaction, peace or inner harmony which you will attain along with the external success attained.

Wherever, your inner peace is sacrificed for an external goal, review your strategy and check whether you want to be unhappier because you want success in a goal set by others and check whether this unhappiness will make you happier in the longer run.

If your sacrifice of short-term peace for success makes you more peaceful in the long run, then only should you choose to sacrifice your peace.

However, if anxiety rises more than the pleasure of success, then you need to change your strategy so that the positive effects of feeling successful remain higher than the negative side effects of the activity pursued.

Success is a tool for attaining more happiness and your reward for being successful needs to be an increasing level of satisfaction and inner happiness.

Do not compromise your soul needs or your self - esteem for money or medals as the money earned and spent; or medals hanging on the wall will not increase your emotional competence while dealing with life's routine problems. Corruption or self-deceit will make you feel more helpless and betrayed by circumstances in the long run. Only an ability to increase your positive soul frequency to be healthier, clearer, confident and more peaceful while making choices, will help you remain competent to face life's challenges in the long run.

Encourage original thinking, creative work and developing awareness of how to work for helping the self than for blind obedience.

Do not imitate hard work which is mechanical as done by oxen. Ox, bulls and donkeys are areas of human intelligence trapped in obedience used by competitive traditions which have led to restlessness in societies.

Do not get trapped into following worker behavior where you feel as if you work like a donkey the whole day and get no more satisfaction than a sack of hay at the end of the day.

Ensure that you feel satisfied or peaceful with every work you do be it hard or simple.

Be aware that imitation would work more than preaching as children learn by observation of adult behavior more than by obeying words which they preach as good values. Hence, avoid preaching behaviors or ethics which you cannot follow yourself on the practical plane.

If you choose to teach traditional values, explain that tradition cannot be blindly obeyed, rules change with circumstances and original thinking may always be needed to cross check on the efficacy of a rule.

Also, children need to be explained that they need not feel sad or guilty of they break rules. Several people retain memories of cheating in childhood and keep feeling sad or repeating patterns of the same behavior as they become habitual to the negative feelings of guilt, remorse and repetition of accidents.

Methods to erase and rescript events where the child feels sad after it's done, need to be used to prevent patterns of repetition of the same behavior. For example, if the child is asked to replay the event in memory and erase it with a rubber, the memory gets literally erased in the subconscious mind. Next, if the child is told to replay the event again and imagine a different outcome, it gets re-scripted in the subconscious mind as a programmer repertoire.

The specific step wise technique for erasing and describing memories is given in my book EMOTIONAL MANAGEMENT.

Avoid making learning easy by making children learn definitions by rote. Children need to be encouraged for grasping and applying concept than for learning the lines. The more children apply rules, the more adults would learn to apply thinking to traditions. By applying the mind to rules and rituals, adults will learn to discard the rules which no longer serve them and thus evolve to happiness with more responsibility.

Exercise 70 (PE 13.10) - Do not teach children to become more anxious than peaceful while pursuing any activity

Teach children to complete tasks with patience and to take breaks wherever needed. Teach them that their peacefulness and interest while doing an activity is more important than completing the task as a boring, routine chore.

Encourage children to prioritize activities and to choose those tasks which they enjoy doing than imitate others for fashion or ritual.

Also, teach the kids to not become anxious if a task is not completed as planned.

Anxiety disorders often result from a mind conditioned into living life as defined by rules. Teaching the kids that everything does not go as planned and obstacles need to be confronted as blessings which lead to soul evolution, is necessary for them to cope up with challenges of adult life with a positive attitude.

An understand of the needs of the inner self and how to address them would be activated by following exercises given in this book .

Conclusion

Failure and success need to be redefined such that children identify success with increasing happiness, peacefulness and good health; while failure is that which leads to unhappiness in self, disharmony in the body and angry temperaments .Failure needs to be treated as feedback than as punishment and methods of overcoming failure need to be pursued with patience and perseverance till success is achieved in a way which creates harmony in all angles. For example, Thomas Edison failed for thirty years before he could devise an electric bulb.

Children need to be taught a process of being successful where individual success leads to success for all. From the soul's perspective, success needs to ensure an ever increasing rise in happiness in the self and in the world, not just in the self at the cost of the world. Students who are encouraged to win by defeating everyone else grow up as competitive adults who feel justified in gaining success at the cost of creating losses for everyone else in the world. .

Till success is simply defined as competitive excellence, it would lead to increase in unrest in society, growth of competitive games, terrorism and disharmony in households.

...For a peaceful world, it is essentially that peaceful children are cultivated with a focus on teaching compassion over competition. The road to success with happiness is longer but it is not empty of fulfilment as success without happiness is.

Success pursued with feeling happy would include teaching children how to meditate , how to be silent on regular intervals for a minute to break negative thinking circuits , how to erase memories and rescript subconscious programmes, how to love & respect themselves without defeating others, how to use self therapeutic processes like inner child healing, energy showers & emotional cord cutting.

These processes are given in my books REDEFINING HAPPINESS

and EMOTIONAL MANAGEMENT and need to be adapted for use by children which will be done in the sequel of this book...

Other than using meditation for short intervals to increase patience, children can be trained into:

- Self -Healing Exercises To Erase Negative Memories
- Self-Healing Exercises To Improve Conflict Understanding
- Self-Healing Exercise To Increase Confidence And Cut Negative Energy Cords
- Self-Healing Exercise To Understand Desires And Heal The Inner Child
- Self-Healing Relaxation Exercise to be Detached from Criticism
- Self-Healing Exercises To Remove Anger On A Daily Basis
- Self-Healing Exercise To Remove Minor Pains By Energy Rotation
- Self-Healing Exercise To Understand Different Perspectives
- Energy Shower Healing
- Praying for a Vibratory Energy Connection With Source of Wisdom and Light

Part 2 of this book will focus in therapeutic exercises for self-help methods for teenagers

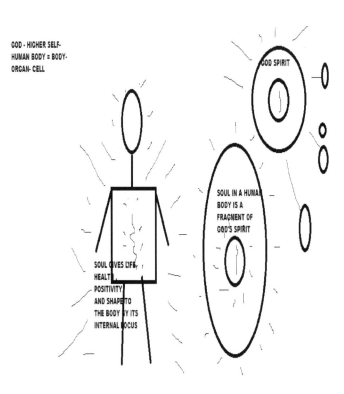

Printed in Poland
by Amazon Fulfillment
Poland Sp. z o.o., Wrocław